W9-BUJ-202

Contents

CHAPTER 1

A Day in the Life

A group of penguins speeds through the sea. The birds' colors help keep them safe. **Predators** in the air can't see the birds' black backs. Predators in the water struggle to see penguins' white bellies.

Flying through the Water

The group moves through the water easily. Penguins don't fly. But their flippers work like wings. Penguins use their flippers to swim and dive.

Quick Breath

Penguins swim just below the water's surface. To breathe, they leap out for half a second. They take a breath. Then they drop back in the water.

7

PENGUIN FEATURES

BLACK OR GRAY BACK

FLIPPERS

BILL

SHORT TAIL

WEBBED FEET

WHITE BELLY

SHORT LEGS

COMPARING SIZES

Little Penguins

15 INCHES
(38 centimeters)

2 POUNDS
(1 kilogram)

Emperor Penguins

45 INCHES
(114 cm)

88 POUNDS
(40 kg)

POUNDS 0

Staying Warm

The water is cold. But penguins' feathers keep them warm. The fat beneath their skin keeps them warm too.

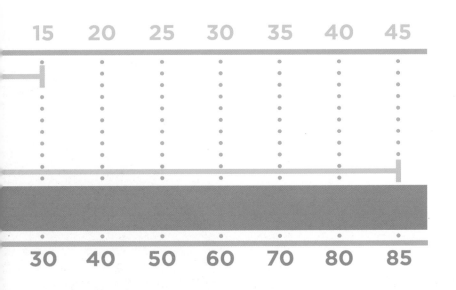

CHAPTER 2

Food to Eat
and a Place to Live

Penguins eat fish, **krill**, and squid. Some swallow small stones. The stones help break up food in their stomachs. Penguins go without eating for 20 or more days each year. They don't eat when it's time to **mate**. They also stop eating when they **molt**.

Diving for Food

Penguins catch all their food in the sea. They dive down to find and catch **prey**. Then they swallow it whole.

There are about 17 types of penguins. Almost all penguins live in the **Southern Hemisphere**. Five types live in Antarctica. The rest live farther north.

A penguin's tongue is covered in sharp spines. The spines help it grip slippery prey.

WHERE PENGUINS LIVE

Penguin Range Map

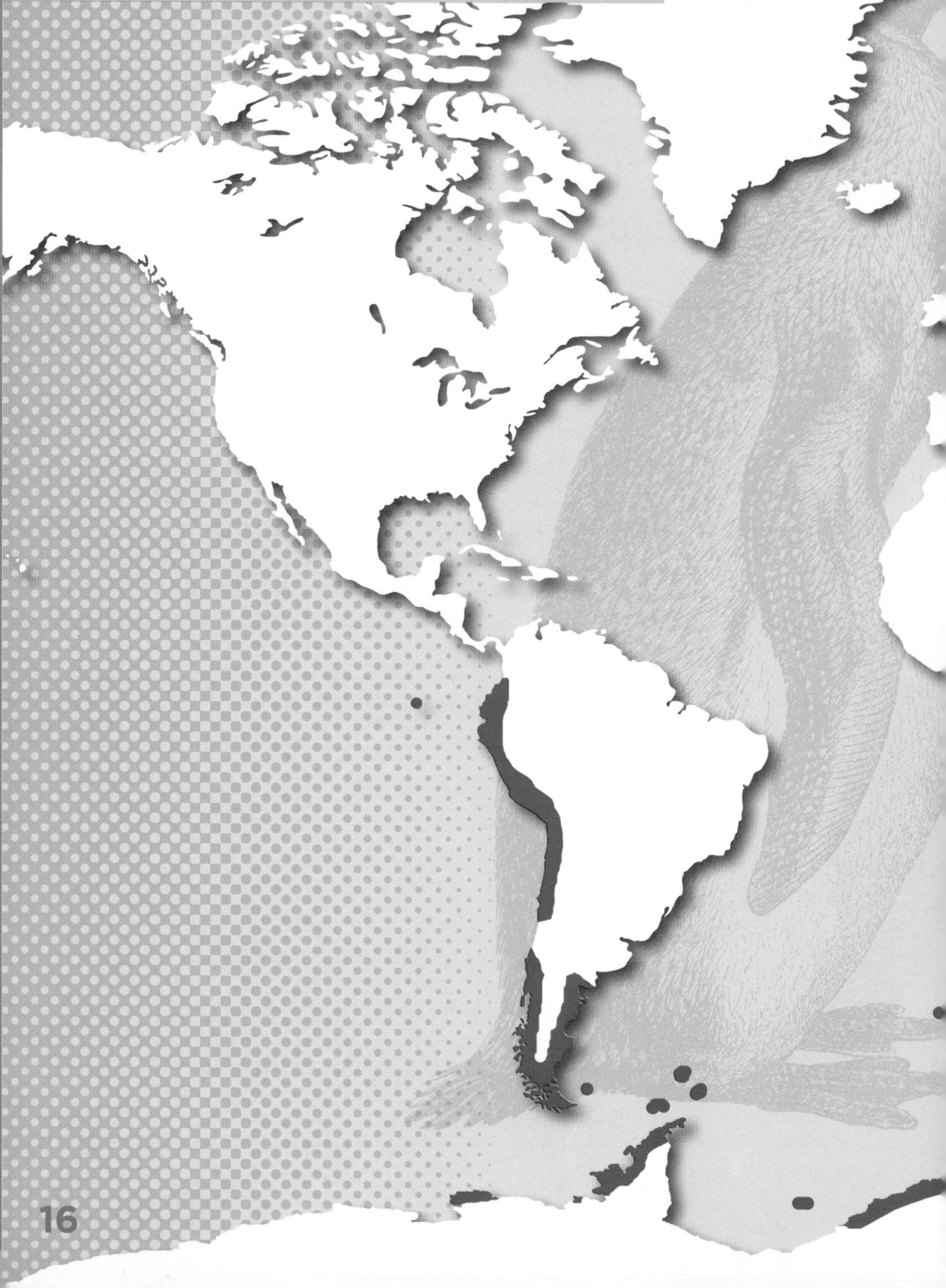

CHAPTER 3

Family Life

Penguins spend most of their time in the water. They come out to mate, lay eggs, and raise chicks. Penguins tend to build nests in the same places each year. And most build nests in large **colonies**. Some colonies have fewer than 100 pairs of penguins. Some have more than 100,000 pairs.

Laying Eggs

Most penguins lay their eggs in spring and summer. King and emperor penguins lay just one egg. They don't build nests. All other penguins lay two eggs in nests.

Types of Penguin Nests

PLATFORM

MADE OF STONES OR TWIGS

BURROW

DUG IN THE GROUND

BOWL

SCRAPED IN THE GROUND AND LINED WITH PLANTS OR STONES

21

Caring for the Young

Penguin parents work together to care for their chicks. They take turns keeping the chicks warm. They take turns hunting too.

When chicks get bigger, both parents hunt at the same time. Chicks wait in huge groups. The parents listen for their chicks when they come back. Each chick has its own call.

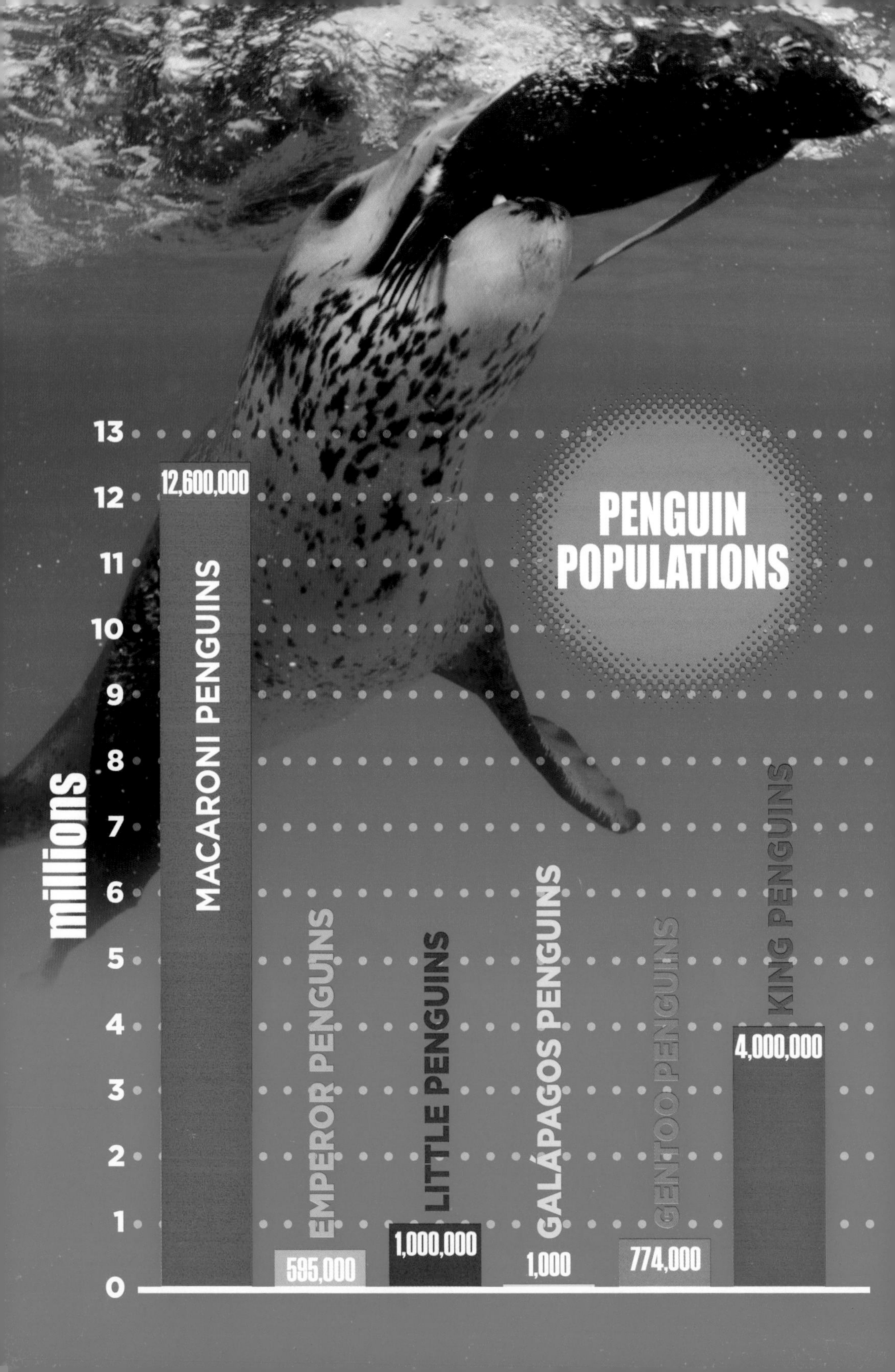

PENGUIN POPULATIONS

millions

13

12 — 12,600,000 — MACARONI PENGUINS

11

10

9

8 — KING PENGUINS

7

6 — GALÁPAGOS PENGUINS

5 — EMPEROR PENGUINS — LITTLE PENGUINS — GENTOO PENGUINS

4 — 4,000,000

3

2

1 — 1,000,000

0 — 595,000 — 1,000 — 774,000

CHAPTER 4

Predators
and Other Threats

Whales, seals, and sea lions are penguins' top threats at sea. On land, adults have few predators. But chicks have a hard time. Sea birds, such as gulls, eat them.

Oil spills from ships are a big problem. Oil coats penguins' feathers. The oil makes it hard for them to keep warm. They also clean their feathers with their beaks. The oil they swallow makes them sick.

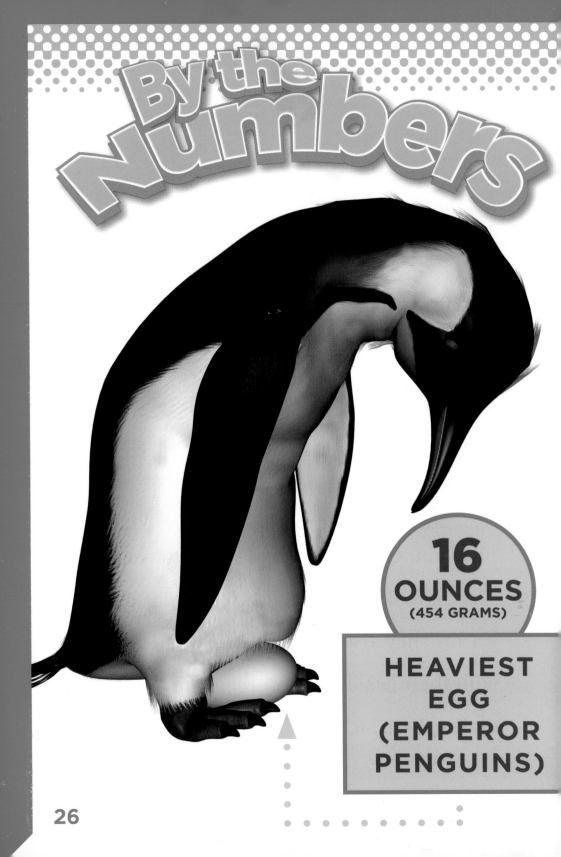

By the Numbers

16 OUNCES (454 GRAMS)

HEAVIEST EGG (EMPEROR PENGUINS)

DEEPEST DIVE
(EMPEROR PENGUINS)

1,854 FEET
(565 METERS)

22
MILES
(35 KILOMETERS)
PER HOUR

FASTEST SWIM SPEED (GENTOO PENGUINS)

15 to 20 YEARS
LIFE SPAN

1,000 PENGUINS

LOWEST WORLD POPULATION (GALÁPAGOS PENGUINS)

Helping Penguins

Some types of penguins are in danger of going extinct. People are trying to help by cleaning up oil spills. Land where some penguins live has been set aside as parks too. The parks give them a safe place to live. All this work helps keep penguins safe.

burrow (BUR-oh)—a hole in the ground made by an animal for shelter or protection

colony (KAH-luh-nee)—a group of animals of the same type living closely together

krill (KRIL)—small shellfish

mate (MAYT)—to join together to produce young

molt (MOLT)—to lose a covering of hair, feathers, or skin and replace it with new growth

predator (PRED-uh-tuhr)—an animal that eats other animals

prey (PRAY)—an animal hunted or killed for food

Southern Hemisphere (SUH-thurn HEM-is-feer)—the southern half of Earth

Books

Esbaum, Jill. *Penguins*. Explore My World. Washington, D.C.: National Geographic Society, 2014.

Franks, Katie. *Penguins*. The Zoo's Who's Who. New York: PowerKids Press, 2015.

Lewis, Suzanne. *A Penguin Named Patience: A Hurricane Katrina Rescue Story*. Ann Arbor, MI: Sleeping Bear Press, 2015.

Websites

Emperor Penguin
kids.nationalgeographic.com/animals/emperor-penguin/

Penguins
www.defenders.org/penguins/basic-facts

Penguins
www.dkfindout.com/us/animals-and-nature/birds/penguins/

INDEX

Wild Animal Kingdom

PENGUINS

GAIL TERP

BLACK
RABBIT
BOOKS

Bolt is published by Black Rabbit Books
P.O. Box 3263, Mankato, Minnesota, 56002.
www.blackrabbitbooks.com
Copyright © 2017 Black Rabbit Books

Design and Production by Michael Sellner
Photo Research by Rhonda Milbrett

Library of Congress Control Number: 2015954839

HC ISBN: 978-1-68072-054-9   PB ISBN: 978-1-68072-311-3

Printed in the United States at CG Book Printers,
North Mankato, Minnesota, 56003. PO #1798 4/16

Web addresses included in this book were working and appropriate at the time of publication. The publisher is not responsible for broken or changed links.

Image Credits
Adobe Stock: andreanita, 19; aussieanouk, 22–23; Alamy: Martin Creasser, 14 (bottom); Corbis: DLILLC, 4–5; Doug Allan/Nature Picture Library, 27 (top); Kimberly Walker, 21 (top); istock: Buenaventur-amariano, 21 (bottom); Nat Geo: PAUL NICKLEN, 10, 24; Shutterstock: Algol, 26; Andrew S. Williams, 14 (top); BMJ, Cover; Christian Musat, 7; David Osborn, 3; Dmytro Pylypenko, 20; Footage.Pro, 18–19; Hein Nou-wens, 16 (background); Kotomiti Okuma, 31; MyImages – Micha, 12–13; prochasson frederic, back cover, 1; Sergey Uryadnikov, 6; Shchipkova Elena, 8–9; sunsinger, 29; Volodymyr Goinyk, 32; Volt Collection, 27 (bottom)
Every effort has been made to contact copyright holders for material reproduced in this book. Any omissions will be rectified in subse-quent printings if notice is given to the publisher.

BETWEEN the APPLE-BLOSSOM & the WATER

BETWEEN the APPLE-BLOSSOM & the WATER

WOMEN WRITING about GARDENS

Edited by PAMELA NORRIS

A SUMMER HERBACEOUS BORDER, *Lilian Stannard*

A Bulfinch Press Book
LITTLE, BROWN AND COMPANY
Boston · New York · Toronto · London

For My Parents

Text and compilation copyright © 1994 by Pamela Norris

First edition

ISBN 0-8212-2139-6

Decorative illustrations by Nadine Wickenden
Designed by David Fordham
Filmset by SX Composing Ltd, Rayleigh, Essex
Please see pages 119–120 for further acknowledgements.

A CIP catalogue record for this book
is available from the British Library
Library of Congress Catalog Card Number 94-70355

Published simultaneously in the United States of America by Bulfinch Press,
an imprint and trademark of Little, Brown and Company (Inc.),
in Great Britain by Little, Brown and Company (UK) Ltd,
and in Canada by Little, Brown & Company (Canada) Limited

PRINTED IN ITALY

CONTENTS

INTRODUCTION

> She walks among the loveliness she made,
> Between the apple-blossom and the water –
> She walks among the patterned pied brocade,
> Each flower her son, and every tree her daughter.

Written by one of the great English gardeners, Vita Sackville-West, these lines from her poem *The Land* emphasize a relationship between women and gardens that is central to this anthology. Published between 1860 and 1935, the gardening books, novels and poems from which the texts have been selected reveal not only a delight in plants and flowers, but also a passion for the making of gardens. For Victorian women, the new enthusiasm for domestic gardening offered an opportunity for activity and pleasure, and the chance to create something of their own in a society where formal employment was considered demeaning for the middle-class woman. Under-occupied and confined to stuffy rooms, women flocked to their gardens as a never-failing source of enjoyment and interest, with the additional bonus of healthy exercise in the welcome fresh air.

Victorian women were not always active participants in garden tasks. As long as male gardeners were cheap and readily available, it was easy to maintain the convention of female weakness. Women's so-called 'tiny' hands and feet, the social myth of their lack of physical strength and intolerance of damp, as well as their hampering and impractical clothes, deterred many from 'unladylike' labour, but they could still engage in the delightful by-products of horticulture. Annie Hassard's manual on flower-arranging brings the garden into the house with sometimes extravagant suggestions for floral display. Edith Chamberlain and Fanny Douglas offer advice on distilling flower scents, while Mrs Richmond gives a wonderful recipe for an old-fashioned potpourri: 'Collect a quantity of the petals of red roses, jasmine, lavender buds, mignonette, and all manner of sweet-scented flowers . . .'.

Frances Wolseley was an enthusiastic supporter of the traditional art of potpourri, but she pooh-poohed the myth of female weakness. Her Glynde College for Lady Gardeners, founded in Sussex in the early 1900s, gave women a tough two-year training in practical gardening and land management. Innovative in her attitude to women's capabilities, Frances also reformed their clothes, and the Glynde gardeners wore a sensible uniform adapted to digging, weeding, and climbing ladders. Her description of appropriate headgear for the garden suggests that she would not have approved of the millinery that appears in many Victorian garden paintings: 'it must be plain, not trimmed with chiffon or flowers.'

A major innovator in English gardening, Gertrude Jekyll proved that women could do anything they set their hands to. Painter, photographer and craftswoman, she insisted on personally mastering such diverse skills as embroidery and smith's work. When she turned to gardening, her painter's eye proved invaluable, and with the publication of her first books on gardening and in particular *Colour in the Flower Garden* (1908), a new concept of colour and planting revolutionized garden design in England and the United States. 'Making Garden Pictures' expresses her philosophy of the visual: one or a few flowering plants 'carefully placed . . . to please the eye and give ease to the mind.' 'Hollyhocks' indicates the fine discrimination with which she appreciated the features of an individual plant. Other writers were less restrained in their approach both to colour and to language. In her breathless 'Indian Visions', E.V.B. promiscuously abandons herself to an uncontrolled riot of scarlet and crimson: 'Indian visions steeped in glory, visions of Delhi and last year's Durbar floated through the fiery brilliance'.

The appropriate cultivation of plants fills many pages of gardening manuals, but Kathleen Murray adds a new twist with her account of rearing French roses in India. The perfume of flowers was almost as important as their colour: Elizabeth von Arnim writes seductively about scented sweet peas, while Eleanour Sinclair Rohde recalls a perfumed garden of her childhood. In her long poem 'The Old Garden', Margaret Deland also writes about an old-fashioned garden, where

 Still from the far-off pastures comes the bee,
And swings all day inside the hollyhock,
Or steals her honey from the winged sweet-pea,
Or the striped glory of the four-o'clock;

A nostalgia for the golden gardens of childhood frequently appears in novels that have become children's classics. In an extract from *Little Women*, Louisa May Alcott describes the gardens of the March girls, where each separate plot defines its owner's character, from the showy Amy with her earwiggy bower, to Meg with her orange tree, symbol of her destiny as a bride. The redoubtable Jane in L. M. Montgomery's 'An Island Garden' has no problem with digging and even manure, but her garden, too, recreates a magical fragrant past: 'There was ribbon-grass and mint, bleeding-heart, prince's feather, southernwood, peonies, sweet balm, sweet may, sweet william, all with sated, velvet bees humming over them.' The garden in Frances Hodgson Burnett's novel, *The Secret Garden*, is associated with a mother's care. Rediscovered by the sour orphan Mary after years of neglect, its restoration to abundant bloom brings about the emotional healing of two neglected and unhappy children.

The recuperative effect of gardening is charmingly evoked by Helena Rutherfurd Ely, whose innovative *A Woman's Hardy Garden* (1903) helped to emancipate her American readers from the constraints of the bedding-out system. Her fellow-countrywoman Louisa King, a founder member of the Garden Club of America, felt that gardening offered social as well as personal benefits, providing an opportunity to share communal activity. As 'An Anglo-American Encounter' indicates, her benevolent generosity was sometimes disappointed.

For many garden-writers, their books acted as a form of journal, a way of sharing opinions and experiences along with practical information on horticulture. Theresa Earle's 'Pot-Pourri' books combine gardening tips, recipes, advice on further reading, views on vegetarianism and the education of daughters, with anecdotes of her daily life. Marion Cran imparts an enormous sense of fun, philosophy and personal courage along with her accounts of budding roses and planting daffodils. Not all the writers stayed at home. The du Canes went to Madeira, Japan and the Canary Islands to collect material for the books that Florence wrote and Ella illustrated, in a series of fine watercolours that are now almost unknown. Vernon Lee's account of the Generalife gardens in Granada explores atmosphere, the *genius loci* or essence of a place that is the subject of many of her traveller's tales.

In the novels of the period, descriptions of gardens and that artificial forcing house for plants, the conservatory, are often essential elements in the action of a story. In 'The Sanctuary', Rhoda Broughton's heroine Margaret takes refuge from a claustrophobic evening party in a tranquil walled garden massed with creepers and autumn flowers. The simple and honest Molly, in Mrs Gaskell's 'A Visit to the Towers Gardens', also suffers from an oppressive social occasion, and escapes from the contrived atmosphere of the hothouse to the fresh open air and beautiful gardens outside. For Maggie and Stephen, in George Eliot's 'Maggie and the Rose', the slow promenade in the enclosed and fervid atmosphere of the conservatory brings their passion to fever pitch. In Sarah Orne Jewett's 'Miss Sydney's Flowers', the life of a narrow and reclusive woman is transformed when the opening of a new street exposes her private conservatory to public view.

Again and again, plants provide metaphors for emotions and character. In Katherine Mansfield's 'The Pear Tree', a pear tree in full blossom becomes a symbol for a young woman's feelings about her life. For Olive Schreiner's Lyndall, love 'is a blood-red flower, with the colour of sin; but there is always the scent of a god about it.' Spring flowers seem to start up in Fernham gardens when Virginia Woolf wanders there one October evening at the magical hour between dusk and dark. In Edith Wharton's 'A Magic Place', the heroine Lily is not only named after the flower that symbolizes purity but resembles it in her 'white-robed slimness' and the flower-like motion of her face.

The depiction of gardens and garden scenes proved to be just as fascinating for the artists of the late Victorian and early twentieth-century period as for the writers, and their approach to the subject is equally diverse. One of the most famous of the garden painters was George Samuel Elgood (1851-1943), a prolific artist who took a strong interest in garden design and painted many of the great Renaissance gardens on his frequent visits to Italy. His enthusiasm for the grand historic English garden led to *Some English Gardens* (1904), in which Elgood's magnificent paintings are supplemented by Gertrude Jekyll's commentary. 'Blyborough, Lincolnshire, 1901' and 'Raundscliffe – Everywhere are Roses' demonstrate his eye for composition, sense of colour and naturalistic style. Elgood's contemporary, the Scottish painter Arthur Claude Strachan (1865-*c.*1935), had rather different interests. Also a highly productive artist, he painted idealized English cottage gardens, with carefully detailed flowers. 'At Dunster' is a charming example of his work.

Among other artists who specialized in garden subjects was Lilian Stannard (1877-1944), who came from a Bedfordshire family of artists. 'A Summer Herbaceous Border' demonstrates her vivid, rather impressionistic approach. The more delicate palette of the Irish artist, Mildred Anne Butler (1858-1941), can be seen in 'Madonna Lilies' and 'A Bypath'. The technique of her fellow-countryman, David Woodlock (1842-1929), was to apply watercolour to wet paper, producing a less precise image than was common with conventional garden painting, but, as can be seen in 'In the Garden' and 'A Cottage Garden at Sunset', the effect is of rich profusion.

As with the novelists, many artists used flowers and gardens as backgrounds to a narrative that is usually left to the viewer to unravel. When a painting is paired with an extract in this book, its meaning can be given a more specific interpretation. John William Waterhouse's 'My Sweet Rose' does not take place in a conservatory, but his voluptuous image seems perfect for George Eliot's tremulous Maggie. 'Choosing', Frederick Watts' painting of his child-bride Ellen Terry, suggests a symbolic dilemma between the vivid camellia held to her nose and the delicate (and sweeter-smelling?) violets clutched to her heart. These contrasts mirror the variations in love outlined in 'A Blood-Red Flower'. Marcel Rieder's 'Reflections' suggests the pensive tranquillity of Ann Bridge's 'After the Storm'.

The differences in technique, subject matter and ways of seeing that appear in these pages reflect the multiplicity of artists and their enthusiasms, and also the huge social change that took place during this period. Just as Bompard's mysterious 'The Poppy Garden' contrasts dramatically with the serene English summer of Walbourn's 'The Garden Path', and the formal precision of Lovmand's 'The Rose Bush' with Templeuve's riotous nasturtiums, so the images of women offer significant differences. Grimshaw's self-conscious study of his wife in 'In the Pleasaunce' and Tissot's elaborately costumed lady posing in her conservatory seem a far cry from Childe Hassam's relaxed image of Celia Thayer, who has escaped from the stifling confines of Victorian corsets and greenhouses to wander at ease in the colourful profusion of her garden.

There are many women gardeners in this anthology, who it is to be hoped similarly found the time to walk at ease among the loveliness that they had made. As writers, they also did their best to create something of their own, a verbal image of the flowers and gardens that they knew or imagined, and that we, their readers, are privileged to share.

> The gorsey common swells a golden sea,
>   The cowslip hangs a head of golden tips,
> And golden drips the honey which the bee
>   Sucks from sweet hearts of flowers and stores and sips.

PAMELA NORRIS
1994

THE SENSUOUS GARDEN

⁂

CUPS OF SCENT

DELICATELY SPILLING

THEMSELVES OVER THEIR

BRIMS AND FILLING THE

GARDEN AIR . . .

IN THE PLEASAUNCE, KNOSTROP OLD HALL, LEEDS,
John Atkinson Grimshaw

THE SCENTED SWEET-PEA

July 1st. – I think that after roses sweet-peas are my favourite flowers. Nobody, except the ultra-original, denies the absolute supremacy of the rose. She is safe on her throne, and the only question to decide is which are the flowers that one loves next best. This I have been a long while deciding, though I believe I knew all the time somewhere deep down in my heart that they were sweet-peas; and every summer when they first come out, and every time going round the garden, that I come across them, I murmur involuntarily, 'Oh yes, *you* are the sweetest, you dear, dear little things.' And what a victory this is, to be ranked next the rose even by one person who loves her garden. Think of the wonderful beauty triumphed over – the lilies, the irises, the carnations, the violets, the frail and delicate poppies, the magnificent larkspurs, the burning nasturtiums, the fierce marigolds, the smooth cool pansies. I have a bed at this moment in the full glory of all these things, . . . where, in the dampest corner, shining in the sun, but with their feet kept cool and wet, is a colony of Japanese irises, and next to them higher on the slope Madonna lilies, so chaste in looks and so voluptuous in smell, and then a group of hollyhocks in tenderest shades of pink, and lemon, and white, and right and left of these white marguerites and evening primroses and that most exquisite of poppies called Shirley, and a little on one side a group of metallic blue delphiniums beside a towering white lupin, and in and out and everywhere mignonette, and stocks, and pinks, and a dozen other smaller but not less lovely plants. I wish I were a poet, that I might properly describe the beauty of this bit as it sparkles this afternoon in the sunshine after rain; but of all the charming, delicate, scented groups it contains, none to my mind is so lovely as the group of sweet-peas in its north-west corner.

ELIZABETH VON ARNIM

AMONG THE FLOWERS, *Robert Payton Reid*

LILIES, DELPHINIUMS AND POPPIES IN THE GARDEN OF THE ARTIST'S COTTAGE, *Edward Kington Brice*

THE REBELLIOUS BORDER

The scarlet poppies of early June introduce a colour that seems to belong with the flowers of mid-summer and appears out of place among the more delicate hues of the early garden even as the scarlet tulip looks gaudy in contrast with the narcissi and iris, though perhaps for well blended richness the hardy flowers of June will match those of any season. The larkspurs ranging from white through sky and mazarine blue to a metallic purple; Canterbury bells of a fine porcelain opaqueness, white, lilac, rose, and purple; columbines of every solid colour and the white-lined varieties, too, that suggest the fairylike blossoms wrought by skilful glass blowers; lemon-yellow day lilies that make a brave showing against a background of copper beech branches; peonies like great roses, beginning in May with the crimson Jacqueminot colour; spires of old-world foxglove, four feet tall, swaying above the golden glow of hardy coreopsis; and mats of sweet William, white, pink, crimson, pheasant's eye, and harlequin, that crowd the fringed clove pinks almost out of the border. Then, too, there is a day edition of the yellow evening primrose, and honesty (lunaria), the herb of magic, in three tints, – white, lavender, and purple.

All these flowers are of course improved by frequent resowing and resetting, and by having ample elbow room, and yet nowhere do they seem so typical, so gracefully lovable, and so wholly what hardy folk should be, as in the bit of the old border that we have not yet disciplined, where the soil is completely hidden by a tangle of poppies, sweet William, and foxgloves.

BARBARA CAMPBELL

LIFE LIKE A WIND

＊━━＊

In a steamer chair, under a manuka tree that grew in the middle of the front grass patch, Linda Burnell dreamed the morning away. She did nothing. She looked up at the dark, close, dry leaves of the manuka, at the chinks of blue between, and now and again a tiny yellowish flower dropped on her. Pretty – yes, if you held one of those flowers on the palm of your hand and looked at it closely, it was an exquisite small thing. Each pale yellow petal shone as if each was the careful work of a loving hand. The tiny tongue in the centre gave it the shape of a bell. And when you turned it over the outside was a deep bronze colour. But as soon as they flowered, they fell and were scattered. You brushed them off your frock as you talked; the horrid little things got caught in one's hair. Why, then, flower at all? Who takes the trouble – or the joy – to make all these things that are wasted, wasted. . . . It was uncanny.

On the grass beside her, lying between two pillows, was the boy. Sound asleep he lay, his head turned away from his mother. His fine dark hair looked more like a shadow than like real hair, but his ear was a bright, deep coral. Linda clasped her hands above her head and crossed her feet. It was very pleasant to know that all these bungalows were empty, that everybody was down on the beach, out of sight, out of hearing. She had the garden to herself; she was alone.

Dazzling white the picotees shone; the golden-eyed marigolds glittered; the nasturtiums wreathed the veranda poles in green and gold flame. If only one had time to look at these flowers long enough, time to get over the sense of novelty and strangeness, time to know them! But as soon as one paused to part the petals, to discover the under-side of the leaf, along came Life and one was swept away. And, lying in her cane chair, Linda felt so light; she felt like a leaf. Along came Life like a wind and she was seized and shaken; she had to go. Oh dear, would it always be so? Was there no escape?

KATHERINE MANSFIELD

✤

GIRL UNDER A PARASOL, *P. Lira*

GREAT-AUNT LANCILLA'S SCENTED GARDEN

When I think of scented gardens I remember hers first and foremost, for though since those days I have seen many gardens, I do not think I have ever seen a pleasanter, homelier one. The house was Georgian, and the short drive to it was flanked on both sides by pollarded lime trees. (I have only to shut my eyes to hear the hum of the bees now.) The drive was never used by the household nor indeed by anyone who came on foot, for the shortest way from the village was through a gate leading from the road to a side door. The path was perfectly straight, and bordered on either side by very broad beds, and except in midwinter they were full of scent and colour. I can see the big bushes of the pale pink China roses and smell their delicate perfume; I see the tall old-fashioned delphiniums and the big red peonies and the clumps of borage, the sweet-williams, the Madonna and tiger lilies and the well-clipped bushes of lad's love. Before the time of roses I remember chiefly the Canterbury bells and pyrethrums, and earlier still the edge nearest the path was thick with wallflowers and daffodils. I have never seen hollyhocks grow as they grew at the back of those borders, and they were all single ones, ranging from pale yellow to the deepest claret. Beyond this path, on one side was the big lawn with four large and very old mulberry trees. As a child it frequently struck me that considering how small mulberries were compared to apples, plums and so forth, it was really little short of a miracle what a glorious mess one could get into with them in next to no time. Amongst the flowers great-aunt Lancilla loved most were evening primroses. I have never since then seen a large border, as she had, entirely given to them. She used to pick the flowers to float in finger bowls at dinner.

ELEANOUR SINCLAIR ROHDE

MADONNA LILIES, *Mildred Anne Butler*

IN THE PARK, *Caroline van Deurs*

WALKING IN KEW GARDENS

From the oval-shaped flower-bed there rose perhaps a hundred stalks spreading into heart-shaped or tongue-shaped leaves half way up and unfurling at the tip red or blue or yellow petals marked with spots of colour raised upon the surface; and from the red, blue or yellow gloom of the throat emerged a straight bar, rough with gold dust and slightly clubbed at the end. The petals were voluminous enough to be stirred by the summer breeze, and when they moved, the red, blue and yellow lights passed one over the other, staining an inch of the brown earth beneath with a spot of the most intricate colour. The light fell either upon the smooth grey back of a pebble, or the shell of a snail with its brown circular veins, or, falling into a raindrop, it expanded with such intensity of red, blue and yellow the thin walls of water that one expected them to burst and disappear. Instead the drop was left in a second silver grey once more, and the light now settled upon the flesh of a leaf, revealing the branching thread of fibre beneath the surface, and again it moved on and spread its illumination in the vast green spaces beneath the dome of the heart-shaped and tongue-shaped leaves. Then the breeze stirred rather more briskly overhead and the colour was flashed into the air above, into the eyes of the men and women who walk in Kew Gardens in July.

VIRGINIA WOOLF

THE OLD GARDEN

Still from the far-off pastures comes the bee,
And swings all day inside the hollyhock,
Or steals her honey from the winged sweet-pea,
Or the striped glory of the four-o'clock;
The pale sweet-william, ringed with pink and white,
Grows yet within the damp shade of the wall;
And there the primrose stands, that as the night
Begins to gather, and the dews to fall,
Flings wide to circling moths her twisted buds,
That shine like yellow moons with pale, cold glow,
And all the air her heavy fragrance floods,
And gives largess to any winds that blow. . . .

Once more I listen for the trembling chime
From purple-throated Canterbury bell;
For surely, in that far-off golden time,
Strange fragrant music from it softly fell.
Beneath the lilacs, on whose heart-shaped leaves
The dust has settled, and white stains of mould,
The money-vine with clinging myrtle weaves
A thick dark carpet, starred with blue and gold.
A wedge of vivid blue the larkspur shines
From out the thorny heart of the sweet-brier,
And at its side are velvet brandy-wines,
Shadowed by honey-suckles' fringe of fire.

Margaret Deland

IN THE GARDEN, *David Woodlock*

THE GARDEN AT ESCRICK HALL, YORKSHIRE, 1921, *Constance Wenlock*

A VISIT TO THE TOWERS GARDENS

Green velvet lawns, bathed in sunshine, stretched away on every side into the finely wooded park; if there were divisions and ha-has between the soft sunny sweeps of grass, and the dark gloom of the forest-trees beyond, Molly did not see them; and the melting away of exquisite cultivation into the wilderness had an inexplicable charm to her. Near the house there were walls and fences; but they were covered with climbing roses, and rare honeysuckles and other creepers just bursting into bloom. There were flower-beds, too, scarlet, crimson, blue, orange; masses of blossom lying on the greensward. Molly held Miss Browning's hand very tight as they loitered about in company with several other ladies, and marshalled by a daughter of the Towers, who seemed half amused at the voluble admiration showered down upon every possible thing and place. Molly said nothing, as became her age and position, but every now and then she relieved her full heart by drawing a deep breath, almost like a sigh. Presently they came to the long glittering range of greenhouses and hothouses, and an attendant gardener was there to admit the party. Molly did not care for this half so much as for the flowers in the open air; but Lady Agnes had a more scientific taste, she expatiated on the rarity of this plant, and the mode of cultivation required by that, till Molly began to feel very tired, and then very faint. She was too shy to speak for some time; but at length, afraid of making a greater sensation if she began to cry, or if she fell against the stands of precious flowers, she caught at Miss Browning's hand, and gasped out –

'May I go back, out into the garden? I can't breathe here!'

'Oh, yes, to be sure, love. I daresay it's hard understanding for you, love; but it's very fine and instructive, and a deal of Latin in it too.'

She turned hastily round not to lose another word of Lady Agnes' lecture on orchids, and Molly turned back and passed out of the heated atmosphere.

ELIZABETH GASKELL

GOLDEN GLORIES

The buttercup is like a golden cup,
  The marigold is like a golden frill,
The daisy with a golden eye looks up,
  And golden spreads the flag beside the rill,
  And gay and golden nods the daffodil,
The gorsey common swells a golden sea,
  The cowslip hangs a head of golden tips,
And golden drips the honey which the bee
  Sucks from sweet hearts of flowers and stores and sips.

CHRISTINA ROSSETTI

SUN AND MOON FLOWERS, *George Dunlop Leslie*

A MEDITERRANEAN GARDEN, *Tom Mostyn*

PERFUMED GARDENS IN MADEIRA

Last, but by no means least in importance, come the sweet-smelling plants, essential to these little miniature gardens. *Olea fragrans*, or sweet olive, also called *Osmanthus fragrans*, must be given the palm, as surely its insignificant little greenish-white flower is the sweetest flower that grows, and fills the whole air with its delicious fragrance. *Diosma ericoides*, a well-named plant – from *dios*, divine, and *osme*, small – ought perhaps to have been given the first place, as it will never fail at every season of the year to bring fragrance to the garden. The tender green of its heath-like growth, when crushed, yields a strong aromatic scent, and no Portuguese garden is complete without its bushes of *Diosma*. If allowed to grow undisturbed, it will make shrubs of considerable size, and in the early spring is covered with little white starry flowers; but as it bears clipping kindly, it is especially dear to the heart of the Portuguese gardener, who will fashion arm-chairs, or tables, or neat round and square bushes, in the same way as the Dutch clip their yew-trees. Rosemary also ranks high in their affections, not only for its sweet-smelling properties, but also because it can be subjected to the same treatment. Sweet-scented verbenas are also favourites, and in spring the tiny white flower of the small creeping smilax suggests the presence of orange-groves by its almost overpowering scent.

FLORENCE DU CANE

Making Garden Pictures

In the case of my own garden, as far as deliberate intention goes, what is aimed at is something quite simple and devoid of complication; generally one thing or a very limited number of flowering things at a time, but that one, or those few things, carefully placed so as to avoid fuss, and to please the eye and give ease to the mind. In many cases the aim has been to show some delightful colour-combination without regard to the other considerations that go to the making of a more ambitious picture. It may be a group in a shrub border, or a combination of border and climbing plants, or some carefully designed company of plants in the rock garden. I have a little rose that I call the Fairy Rose. It came to me from a cottage garden, and I have never seen it elsewhere. It grows about a foot high and has blush-pink flowers with the colour deepening to the centre. In character the flower is somewhere between the lovely Blush Boursault at its best and the little De Meaux. It is an inch and a half across and of beautiful form, especially in the half-opened bud. Wishing to enjoy its beauty to the utmost, and to bring it comfortably within sight, I gave it a shelf in raised rock-work and brought near and under it a clear pale lilac Viola and a good drift of *Achillea umbellata*. It was worth doing. Another combination that gives me much pleasure is that of the pink Pompon Rose Mignonette with Catmint and whitish foliage, such as Stachys or *Artemisia stelleriana*.

GERTRUDE JEKYLL

A HERBACEOUS BORDER, *Hugh L. Norris*

INDIAN VISIONS

❧⟶≈≈⟵❧

Is it not rather tiring this idea of the planning of garden effects, and so long before the time? How many sorts of things tire one! So many books one reads: so many people one sees! So often also long descriptions of well arranged colours in a garden, where all the colours come just right. I am afraid the colours here come very often wrong. That does not pain me much – I merely feel 'the flowers chose to do it, it is no fault of mine.' And if they are happy, what matter though pink does at times mass unkindly against magenta, or if two different lilacs clash, or even if scarlet and crimson come together? Dear flowers! we know they can never look really wrong, or like a mistake, as so often bad contrasts in women's gear. We only say to ourselves or the gardener when flower colours come very much amiss, 'It is unfortunate!' That is all. Crimson and scarlet by choice would hardly mass together. Therefore there was sorrow when a grand glow of scarlet oriental Poppy began to flame round the dazzling crimson of Carmine Pillar, most brilliant of red Roses. But when I began to speak this thought, and to say besides that of course another season the Poppies would have to be moved away somewhere else, the remark of a visitor in the garden opened my eyes as with the force of revelation. 'Is there not,' he said, 'a certain barbaric pomp about so strange a contrast?' The hint was enough. When I looked again, what Indian visions steeped in glory, visions of Delhi and last year's Durbar floated through the fiery brilliance of those border flowers. I think the Poppies will *not* be moved. That very day their great silken petals began to fall, and wind and weather scattered them away.

E.V.B.

THE POPPY GARDEN, *Maurice Bompard*

THE GARDEN PATH, *Ernest Walbourn*

THE SECRET GARDEN BLOOMS

Oh! the things which happened in that garden! . . . At first it seemed that green things would never cease pushing their way through the earth, in the grass, in the beds, even in the crevices of the walls. Then the green things began to show buds, and the buds begun to unfurl and show colour, every shade of blue, every shade of purple, every tint and hue of crimson. In its happy days flowers had been tucked away into every inch and hole and corner. Ben Weatherstaff had seen it done and had himself scraped out mortar from between the bricks of the wall and made pockets of earth for lovely clinging things to grow on. Iris and white lilies rose out of the grass in sheaves, and the green alcoves filled themselves with amazing armies of the blue and white flower lances of tall delphiniums or columbines or campanulas.

'She was main fond o' them – she was,' Ben Weatherstaff said. 'She liked them things as was allus pointin' up to th' blue sky, she used to tell. Not as she was one o' them as looked down on th' earth – not her. She just loved it but she said as th' blue sky allus looked so joyful.'

The seeds Dickon and Mary had planted grew as if fairies had tended them. Satiny poppies of all tints danced in the breeze by the score, gaily defying flowers which had lived in the garden for years, and which it might be confessed seemed rather to wonder how such new people had got there. And the roses – the roses! Rising out of the grass, tangled round the sun-dial, wreathing the tree trunks, and hanging from their branches, climbing up the walls and spreading over them with long garlands falling in cascades – they came alive day by day, hour by hour. Fair fresh leaves, and buds – and buds – tiny at first but swelling and working Magic until they burst and uncurled into cups of scent delicately spilling themselves over their brims and filling the garden air.

FRANCES HODGSON BURNETT

FOCUS ON FLOWERS

THE MYSTERIOUS AGENCIES OF SUNLIGHT, TEXTURE AND LOCAL COLOUR . . .

AT DUNSTER, *Arthur Claude Strachan*

THE ISLAND

She walks among the loveliness she made,
Between the apple-blossom and the water –
She walks among the patterned pied brocade,
Each flower her son, and every tree her
    daughter.
This is an island all with flowers inlaid,
A square of grassy pavement tessellated;
Flowers in their order blowing as she bade,
And in their company by her created.
The waving grasses freckle sun with shade,
The wind-blown waters round the kingcups
    ripple,
Colour on colour chequered and arrayed,
Shadow on light in variable stipple.
Her regiments at her command parade,
Foot-soldier primrose in his rank comes
    trooping,
Then wind-flowers in a scarlet loose brigade,
Fritillary with dusky orchis grouping.
They are the Cossacks, dim in ambuscade,
Scarfed in their purple like a foreign stranger,

Piratical, and apt for stealthy raid,
Wherever's mystery or doubtful danger.
Iris salutes her with his broad green blade,
And marches by with proud imperial pennant,
And tulips in a flying cavalcade
Follow valerian for their lieutenant.
The Lords-and-Ladies dressed for masquerade
In green silk domino discreetly hooded,
Hurry towards the nut-trees' colonnade,
Philandering where privacy's well wooded;
They're the civilians of this bold crusade,
The courtiers of this camp by blossom tented,
With woodbine clambering the balustrade,
And all by briar roses battlemented.
There, in the sunlit grasses green as jade,
She walks; she sees her squadrons at attention,
And, laughing at her flowery escapade,
Stretches her hands towards her dear invention.

VITA SACKVILLE-WEST

SUMMER, 1917, *Harold Harvey*

A BYPATH, *Mildred Anne Butler*

An Embarrassment of Daffodils

With all my passion for bulb planting, I am fain to confess that I became weary once. I saw an advertisement of daffodils, 'fine mixed varieties,' to be had at ten shillings a sack (a sack!) from the Channel Islands; this was, of course, in the sumptuous, pre-war days. I ordered four sacks, and when they arrived found myself with hundreds and hundreds of rather small daffodil bulbs to plant. I had read of the correct way to arrange them in planting so that they should look natural and not stiff and formal, which is to throw them out and plant them as they fall – and that I essayed to do. I alone with my trowel. Anyone who has tried a similar feat of 'naturalisation' will know about how many bulbs I put in the first day, and how sore was the middle of my right palm.

When I shovelled the residue laboriously back into the sacks at eventide and stole sorrowfully home, I felt that the miracle of the loaves and fishes had enacted itself all over again, for though I was persuaded I had planted millions and trillions of daffodils since breakfast, I had nearly four sacks full still left over. Next day I dug out large tracts of turf and planted the bulbs much more quickly in large groups, covering them over afterwards with the turf again; my abounding enthusiasm had been compelled to realise that single holes dug single-handed with a trowel and a blistered palm would never see the end of that job. And even so with this improved method it took a very long time to get them all in. I have never tried buying cheap bulbs since that effort, for only a very small percentage flowered, though the wide scape of grey-green blades that shot up bore eloquent witness to the labour spent on them. Nowadays in like circumstances I plant with a bulb planter, which is a highly satisfactory instrument supplied by all the principal nurserymen; it lifts out a circular piece of soil and turf and as easily replaces it, leaving no mark; and it may be had in several sizes.

MARION CRAN

GARDENS FOR LITTLE WOMEN

As spring came on, a new set of amusements became the fashion, and the lengthening days gave long afternoons for work and play of all sorts. The garden had to be put in order, and each sister had a quarter of the little plot to do what she liked with. Hannah used to say: 'I'd know which each of them gardings belonged to, ef I see 'em in Chiny;' and so she might, for the girls' tastes differed as much as their characters. Meg's had roses and heliotrope, myrtle, and a little orange tree in it. Jo's bed was never alike two seasons, for she was always trying experiments; this year it was to be a plantation of sunflowers, the seeds of which cheerful and aspiring plant were to feed 'Aunt Cockle-top' and her family of chicks. Beth had old-fashioned, fragrant flowers in her garden: sweet peas 'and mignonette, larkspur, pinks, pansies, and southern-wood, with chickweed for the bird and catnip for the pussies. Amy had a bower in hers – rather small and earwiggy, but very pretty to look at – with honeysuckles and morning glories hanging their coloured horns and bells in graceful wreaths all over it; tall white lilies, delicate ferns, and as many brilliant, picturesque plants as would consent to blossom there.

LOUISA MAY ALCOTT

GIRL READING, *Charles Edward Perugini*

HOLLYHOCKS

The loosely-folded inner petals of the loveliest Hollyhocks invite a wonderful play and brilliancy of colour. Some of the colour is transmitted through the half-transparency of the petal's structure, some is reflected from the neighbouring folds; the light striking back and forth with infinitely beautiful trick and playful variation, so that some inner regions of the heart of a rosy flower, obeying the mysterious agencies of sunlight, texture and local colour, may tell upon the eye as pure scarlet; while the wide outer petal, in itself generally rather lighter in colour, with its slightly waved surface and gently frilled edge, plays the game of give and take with light and tint in quite other, but always delightful, ways.

GERTRUDE JEKYLL

BLYBOROUGH, LINCOLNSHIRE, 1901, *George Samuel Elgood*

❧

THE PEAR ORCHARD, *Alfred Parsons*

❧

THE PEAR TREE

She went into the drawing-room and lighted the fire; then, picking up the cushions, one by one, that Mary had disposed so carefully, she threw them back on to the chairs and the couches. That made all the difference; the room came alive at once. As she was about to throw the last one she surprised herself by suddenly hugging it to her, passionately, passionately. But it did not put out the fire in her bosom. Oh, on the contrary!

The windows of the drawing-room opened on to a balcony overlooking the garden. At the far end, against the wall, there was a tall, slender pear tree in fullest, richest bloom; it stood perfect, as though becalmed against the jade-green sky. Bertha couldn't help feeling, even from this distance, that it had not a single bud or a faded petal. Down below, in the garden beds, the red and yellow tulips, heavy with flowers, seemed to lean upon the dusk.

A grey cat, dragging its belly, crept across the lawn, and a black one, its shadow, trailed after. The sight of them, so intent and so quick, gave Bertha a curious shiver.

'What creepy things cats are!' she stammered, and she turned away from the window and began walking up and down. . . .

How strong the jonquils smelled in the warm room. Too strong? Oh, no. And yet, as though overcome, she flung down on a couch and pressed her hands to her eyes.

'I'm too happy – too happy!' she murmured.

And she seemed to see on her eyelids the lovely pear tree with its wide open blossoms as a symbol of her own life.

KATHERINE MANSFIELD

FRENCH ROSES IN AN INDIAN GARDEN

Directly the pruning was over the roots were opened, and very old manure from the cow-shed was put in; then they were closed at once, and to-morrow they will be watered. Again the *mali* disapproved. He wanted to leave the roots exposed to the air for ten days, because, he assured me, this is the *dustoor*.* It is a custom I do not like at all, and I feel sure that the rose bushes like it no better than I do. I can well imagine them nodding their stems to one another, and saying in little shocked whispers, 'They do these things better in France.' For most of my plants came from a 'roseraie' near Lyons, though they appear to like the climate of India very well, and flowered most obligingly the first year I put them down. They were piteous-looking little things when they arrived by post, forty in a torpedo-shaped parcel, with their stems clipped to a foot long, and no earth on their poor bare roots. Acting under instructions from one who knew, I plunged them at once into a thick mud bath, and planted them in new soil in a shaded place. In a fortnight there were leaf buds on the dingy mud-cased stems and soon they were in a glory of leaves, with little tentative buds opening shyly into a new world. They were tiny flowers at first, but of beautiful delicate colours, and as the cold weather went on – for they arrived in November – the blossoms grew bigger and of better form. At the end of their first year I planted them out in the rose walk with my other roses, and now they are acclimatized, and seem on very good terms with their sisters from Lucknow.

KATHLEEN L. MURRAY

*Custom

THE ROSE BUSH, *Christine Marie Lovmand*

A PRETTY COTTAGE GARDEN, *Alfred Augustus Glendening*

AN OLD-FASHIONED GARDEN

January 3rd. – I will begin by telling you that I was brought up for the most part in the country, in a beautiful, wild, old-fashioned garden. This garden, through circumstances, had remained in the hands of an old gardener for more than thirty years, which carries us back nearly a century. Like so many young people I see about me now, I cared only for the flowers growing, that I might have the pleasure of picking them. Mr. Ruskin says that it is luxurious and pleasure-loving people who like them gathered. Gardening is, I think, essentially the amusement of the middle-aged and old. The lives of the young, as a rule, are too full to give the time and attention required.

Almost all that has remained in my mind of my young days in this garden is how wonderfully the old man kept the place. He succeeded in flowering many things year after year with no one to help him, and with the frost in the valley to contend against in spring. It was difficult, too, for him to get seeds or plants, since the place was held by joint owners, whom he did not like to ask for them. The spot was very sheltered, and that is one of the greatest of all secrets for plant cultivation. An ever-flowing mill-stream ran all round the garden; and the hedges of China-roses, Sweetbriar, Honeysuckle, and white Hawthorn tucked their toes into the soft mud, and throve year after year. The old man was a philosopher in his way, and when on a cold March morning my sisters and I used to rush out after lessons and ask him what the weather was going to be, he would stop his digging, look up at the sky, and say: 'Well, miss, it may be fine and it may be wet; and if the sun comes out, it will be warmer.' After this solemn announcement he would wipe his brow and resume his work, and we went off, quite satisfied, to our well-known haunts in the Hertfordshire woods, to gather Violets and Primroses for our mother, who loved them.

THERESA EARLE

BLUE-BELLS IN THE SHADE

The choicest buds in Flora's train, let other fingers twine;
Let others snatch the damask rose, or wreath the eglantine;
I'd leave the sunshine and parterre, and seek the woodland glade,
To stretch me on the fragrant bed of blue-bells in the shade.

Let others cull the daffodil, the lily soft and fair;
And deem the tulip's gaudy cup most beautiful and rare;
But give to me, oh, give to me the coronal that's made
Of ruby orchis mingled with the blue-bells from the shade.

The sunflower and the peony, the poppy bright and gay,
Have no alluring charms for me, I'd fling them all away:
Exotic bloom may fill the vase, or grace the high-born maid;
But sweeter far to me than all, are blue-bells in the shade.

ELIZA COOK

SPRINGTIME IN THE WOODS, *George Henry*

CHARACTER IN FLOWERS

Trees and flowers have also distinct personal character which from time immemorial suggested emblematic significance.

The vulgar names of flowers are always hints of their natural expression, and we relinquish these common names and all that charm of their poetical insight, only because they are not found in seedsmen's catalogues. Buying and selling does take the poetry out of things.

Love-in-a-Mist, Heart's-ease, Baby's Eyes, Redhotpoker, Love-lies-bleeding, Forget-me-not, Snapdragon, Foxglove, Quaker Girls, Snake's-head-Fritillary, Nightshade, Toadstool, Honeysuckle, Traveller's Joy. Are not these names so many witnesses to character? Any one who tends his garden, and knows each plant, recognises very soon indeed that they have a strong determination to move toward a place they fancy, or of protest against their surroundings, with gestures of sorrow and despair. The friendly gardener never hesitates to read these signs and to move the sufferer, no matter what the season. I have even lifted a whole bed of bush hybrid Tea-roses after their buds were formed, and replanted them more favourably without losing a leaf or a Rose. When we see that flowers need us and call for help, we care for them to infatuation, we study their unaccountable fancies, and protect the weak from the strong encroaching bounders; and it is only by their expression and appearance that we know their wants.

The most villainous of bounders are the tribe of Compositae, and, as we should expect, they have little natural beauty of form. Their blooms are agglomerate hard heads. A many-headed mob, like most corporate bodies devoid of conscience, they romp and riot over their refined neighbours.

ANNA LEA MERRITT

ASLEEP AMONG THE FOXGLOVES, *Sidney Shelton*

A FLOWERY GLADE, *Alfred Parsons*

THE ACCOMMODATING RHODODENDRON

My old Munshi in Scinde sent me a present of shikar one day that he had shot in Godap, on the edge of the desert. It was a cheap gift, as it consisted of two hares – unclean animals, which of course he, as a good Mohammedan, could not touch, nor could they be eaten in any self-respecting India Civil Service official's house. In the wondrous letter that accompanied them, a triumph of Indian-English, he informed me that, 'One shot in A.M. will, I think, mach the breakfast time, and the one shot in the P.M. can be used at any time. I have tied a tacket to the leg of one shot in evening.'

Now Rhododendrons are somewhat like Munshi Mahmud's P.M. hare; they may be used at any time and anywhere, dear, accommodating people. For if a gap has to be filled, Rhododendrons can be lifted even in the midst of Summer to fill it, as their roots do not spread far, and with plentiful waterings they will grow on as if they had never been disturbed. Bewildering in variety, scarlet, crimson, white, pink, and purple, Rhododendrons are an absolute necessity in every garden, large or small; not only for their glory of colour in May and June, but for the shelter they afford where shelter is required, for their perfect hardiness, for their immunity from the errant rabbit's teeth, and their generally accommodating ways, suiting themselves to almost any soil, aspect, or climate. When to these we add the flame and gold of hardy Azaleas, it seems as if colour in the modern shrubbery could indeed go no further.

ROSE G. KINGSLEY

MISS SYDNEY'S FLOWERS

The side of her conservatory was now close upon the sidewalk, and this certainly was not agreeable. She could not think of putting on her big gardening-apron, and going in to work among her dear plants any more, with all the world staring in at her as it went by. John the coachman, who had charge of the greenhouse, was at first very indignant; but, after he found that his flowers were noticed and admired, his anger was turned into an ardent desire to merit admiration, and he kept his finest plants next the street. It was a good thing for the greenhouse, because it had never been so carefully tended; and plant after plant was forced into luxuriant foliage and blossom. He and Miss Sydney had planned at first to have close wire screens made to match those in the dining-room; but now, when she spoke of his hurrying the workmen, whom she supposed had long since been ordered to make them, John said, 'Indeed, mum, it would be the ruin of the plants shutting out the light; and they would all be rusted with the showerings I gives them every day.' And Miss Sydney smiled, and said no more.

The street was opened late in October, and, soon after, cold weather began in real earnest. Down in that business part of the city it was the strangest, sweetest surprise to come suddenly upon the long line of blooming plants and tall green lily-leaves under a roof festooned with roses and trailing vines. For the first two or three weeks, almost everybody stopped, if only for a moment. Few of Miss Sydney's own friends even had ever seen her greenhouse; for they were almost invariably received in the drawing-room. Gentlemen stopped the thought of business affairs, and went on down the street with a fresher, happier feeling. And the tired shop-girls lingered longest. Many a man and woman thought of some sick person to whom a little handful of the green leaves and bright blossoms, with their coolness and freshness, would bring so much happiness.

SARAH ORNE JEWETT

IN THE CONSERVATORY, *Jacques Joseph Tissot*

THE PRACTICAL GARDENER

❧━⊷ᴍ⊶━❧

KEEP CAREFUL RECORD OF
ALL OPERATIONS, WITH
EVENTUAL RESULTS, FOR
FUTURE GUIDANCE . . .

A COTTAGE GARDEN, *John Horner*

PETER LEARNS TO BUD ROSES

The laddie dangled the long branch of Marcia in one hand, fumbling in his pocket for the precious knife. I caught the look in his eye, which gave me a reminiscent pang: rather the look of one about to visit the dentist. . . .

'I think I'll just watch you do one first; just once more!' So off we march to the next briar, and I carefully cut the back of the top shoot into an elegant T. We select a nice broad piece of bast, which feels refreshingly wet as I put one end in my mouth to have it ready since both hands are busy. Then he watches me cut out with infinite care the eye of the rose I have chosen, a trusty old friend, Ophelia, to wit, and he watches the way I hold the rose spray, the switchback cut-out, and then the crafty little flick which takes out the bark and leaves the small essential heart glistening sappily on the under side of the slip of bark. That nice wet look cheers both our hearts, we know very well that a dry bud is not a good 'taker.' The sap under the T cut on the wild briar waiting beside us for its great transformation will run slick and easily into the sappy heart of this Ophelia bud and make it swell and grow and yield us sweet harvests of leaf and flower. Peter gazes while I slip the thin ivory end of the budding knife under the T cut in the briar bark, and then run the new bud under the lifted edges, closing the cross-cut at the top of the T comfortably together and quickly binding up briar and bud with the broad wetted bast strip I have been holding ready between my teeth.

Then we place the stool firmly beside his chosen briar, and Peter starts to bud his first rose while I considerately go away to the farthest part of the briar plantation.

MARION CRAN

PRUNING ROSES, *Robert James Gordon*

FEEDING THE DOVES, *Edmond Alphonse Defonte*

THE GARDEN UNCONSTRAINED

In a garden there should be no gloom, no dulness, no damp, neglected spot. There, all should be brightness and delight, and at every turn a surprise, an interest, something unexpected. And from between trim yew hedges and spaces of sunlit lawn, your steps should follow ever some gentle reach of terrace, or winding grass-walk into orchard or hazel close, or wilderness of cedarn shade and hawthorn and young beech, aglow in their season about the roots of them with orange berberis and periwinkle. And there should be no stern master gardener; but one who knows how to deal tenderly with all his children, and how to *let them be*. And then, almost unawares will come patches of the sweetest things, self-sown about the borders, looking secure and happy. Little companies of white violets in spring, will surprise you ever and anon with their perfumed freshness. Many-coloured primroses will smile at you as they nestle at a rose-bush root. Forget-me-not and wood-strawberries, and little lilac gems of Virginian stock, will shelter under your old walls, and none will say them nay. No rough hand essays to check the briony if it choose by chance to clasp some tall tree-stem. Only to that lovely criminal, the bind-weed, would we be cruel. She, alas! must be firmly repressed, or she would soon overmaster us. The plants in such a garden, like living sentient beings, seem to know that all are welcome. They and the gardener understand one another, and there reigns amongst them peace and prosperity.

The birds too are 'let be,' and every bit of harm they do is repaid a hundred-fold by the joy of their song, and the life their merry manners impart to the garden.

E.V.B.

THE GENTLE ART OF DISTILLATION

Before proceeding further, it may perhaps be as well to explain for those who do not understand it the gentle art of distillation. The object of distillation is to separate a desired liquid from undesired impurities – whether liquid or solid – by the aid of heat. Take lavender, for instance. You wish to steal and retain its perfume before the flower dies and withers, and this you can best do by means of distillation. In distillation there are three stages: first, you transform your original substance – which if not liquid must be made liquid by means of heat – into a vapour; next, you turn your vapour, by means of a cooling apparatus, called a condenser, into a liquid again; and, lastly, you catch and retain the new liquid in a vessel called a receiver. At first the advantages of this process are not apparent. What, asks the indignant reader, is the use of turning a liquid into a vapour, and then back to a liquid again? But the principle of the art is this – the perfume that we covet is carried by the flowers in tiny, almost invisible sacs or bags. Steep these flowers in water, apply heat to them, and the perfume, being a volatile (the word explains itself) oil, escapes from the control of the flower, and takes the form of a vapour. The other portions of the plant, being less volatile, remain behind, and we have what we want, the perfume separated from its less essential and interesting companions. The vapour is passed at once into a condenser, kept cool by a stream of water, where it regains its liquid form, and trickles thence into the receiver, to be bottled off for use.

EDITH L. CHAMBERLAIN AND FANNY DOUGLAS

THE BEY'S GARDEN, 1865, *John Frederick Lewis*

GARDENING TOOLS FOR CHILDREN

It is important that the children should be provided with proper tools. I much doubt whether good small tools can be bought ready-made. What are kept in ironmongers' shops as 'ladies tools,' with varnished handles and blue blades, and that are usually given to children, are wretched things, – badly shaped, badly balanced, and generally weak where they should be strongest. The tools should be made by a clever country blacksmith, and the handles carefully adapted to the use of the little hands; perfectly smooth but not varnished. The smallest size of the well-made steel rakes that are sold ready-made will do, but the handle will have to be replaced by a thinner, lighter one.

The necessary tools are spade, rake, hoe, a little wooden trug-basket, and a blunt weeding-knife; a good cutting-knife, a trowel, a hand-fork, and a little barrow. There will also be wanted some raffia for tying, some hazel sticks, and a little white paint. A tiny tool-shed, with a well-lighted fixed bench, is most desirable, the tools hanging in their proper places on the wall. Tools should never be put away dirty. A little wooden implement, that any child can whittle for himself, should be kept on the bench for scraping off any earth that sticks to spade or trowel. The gardener will show you how to make it. A birch broom will also be wanted.

GERTRUDE JEKYLL

THE LITTLE GARDENER, *Harold Swanwick*

TENDING THE NASTURTIUMS, *A. Templeuve*

THE ESSENTIAL GARDENING HAT

In summer, a shady, thick straw hat looks best. It should not be 'floppy,' as this is troublesome in windy weather, and it must be plain, not trimmed with chiffon or flowers. A bit of ribbon round it is all that is wanted. Although a sun-bonnet is picturesque, it is hot and close, for it keeps off the air as well as the sun. The old-fashioned plan of putting a couple of cabbage leaves in the crown of the hat is not to be despised, should the heat be felt very much. For winter, a soft felt hat or cap will be required.

FRANCES GARNET WOLSELEY

THE BULBS ARRIVE

❧━━━◆━━━❧

September 1st. – Postcard from the station announces arrival of parcel, that I at once identify as bulbs, with accompanying Fibre, Moss, and Charcoal mixture. Suggest that Robert should fetch them this afternoon, but he is unenthusiastic, and says to-morrow, when he will be meeting Robin and school-friend, will do quite well.

(*Mem.:* Very marked difference between the sexes is male tendency to procrastinate doing practically everything in the world except sitting down to meals and going up to bed. Should like to purchase little painted motto: *Do it now,* so often on sale at inferior stationers' shops, and present it to Robert, but on second thoughts quite see that this would not conduce to domestic harmony, and abandon scheme at once.)

Think seriously about bulbs, and spread sheets of newspaper on attic floor to receive them and bowls. Resolve also to keep careful record of all operations, with eventual results, for future guidance. Look out notebook for the purpose, and find small green booklet, with mysterious references of which I can make neither head nor tail, in own handwriting on two first pages. Spend some time in trying to decide what I could have meant by: Kp. p. in sh. twice p. w. *without fail* or: Tell H. *not* 12″ by 8″ Washable f.c. to be g'd, but eventually give it up, and tear out two first pages of little green book, and write BULBS and to-morrow's date in capital letters.

September 2nd. – Robert brings home Robin, and friend called Micky Thompson, from station, but has unfortunately forgotten to call for the bulbs.

E. M. DELAFIELD

❧

PICKING HYACINTHS, SPRINGTIME, *Arthur Herbert Buckland*

RAUNDSCLIFFE – EVERYWHERE ARE ROSES, *George Samuel Elgood*

A TRADITIONAL POTPOURRI

The following is an excellent recipe for potpourri as it was made a century ago, which will retain its fragrance for many years. Collect a quantity of the petals of red roses, jasmine, lavender buds, mignonette, and all manner of sweet-scented flowers, and strew them in a cardboard tray, sprinkling them with salt, and drying them in a shady room for a week. Also pluck the leaves of lemon verbena, sweetbriar, mint, rosemary, balm of Gilead, knotted marjoram, sweet basil, lemon, thyme, bay, and other fragrant plants, salting and drying them in the same manner. Then place them in a jar with a close cover, strewing each layer with the following spices, first mixed together: 2 ounces each of cinnamon, cloves, pounded allspice, storax, orris-root (sliced), Calamus aromaticus, gum benjamine, sandalwood shavings, and a small quantity of musk (this is very expensive, and may be omitted), the rind of two lemons, cut thin and sliced as for marmalade, 1 lb. common salt, and a few drops of oil of bergamot or oil of lavender, stirring the compound well together before use. More flowers and leaves can be added as procurable, always drying and salting them first for one week before adding them to the rest. The contents of the jar should be thoroughly mixed and stirred together daily for six weeks, taking care that the spices do not all lie at the bottom of the jar, after which the potpourri is ready for use. Half of it may be used at one time with advantage, keeping the other still closed and occasionally stirred, and changing the contents of the jar and those of the china bowl which contains the potpourri in use occasionally. Fresh salt may always be added, also a few drops of eau de Cologne, lavender-water, or any fragrant essence, if the potpourri should become too dry, with lemon peel, too. The bowl should be covered at night, if possible, to keep in the scent of the potpourri, and prevent dust in it.

More rose petals, lavender, sweet verbena leaves, &c., can be added year by year for a long time, always drying and salting them before adding them to the potpourri.

MRS RICHMOND

I TEND MY FLOWERS FOR THEE

I tend my flowers for thee –
Bright Absentee!
My Fuchsia's Coral Seams
Rip – while the Sower – dreams –

Geraniums – tint – and spot –
Low Daisies – dot –
My Cactus – splits her Beard
To show her throat –

Carnations – tip their spice –
And Bees – pick up –
A Hyacinth – I hid –
Puts out a Ruffled Head –
And odors fall
From flasks – so small –
You marvel how they held –

Globe Roses – break their satin flake –
Upon my Garden floor –
Yet – thou – not there –
I had as lief they bore
No Crimson – more –

Thy flower – be gay –
Her Lord – away!
It ill becometh me –
I'll dwell in Calyx – Gray –
How modestly – alway –
Thy Daisy –
Draped for thee!

EMILY DICKINSON

78

THE HERBACEOUS BORDER, *Alfred John Billinghurst*

FLOWERS ON THE TERRACE, *Victor Gilsoul*

AN ANGLO-AMERICAN ENCOUNTER

Mr. Eden Philpotts brings all the beauty of his poetic style to bear upon the subject of 'My Garden,' thus deliciously prefacing his book: 'The time has come when, to have a garden, and not to write about it, is to be notorious.' Let me commend the three chapters on the iris in this fascinating book to the attention of all iris-lovers. There never has been, there never can come from another pen, so poetic, so beautiful a bit of writing on this alluring flower. Done in entrancing language, it tempts the most unyielding to become an iris-collector. I myself, on reading these descriptions, felt so deep a debt of gratitude to Mr. Philpotts for them, and for the pleasure which for years back had been given me by his Devonshire tales, that I experienced a real delight when the following request caught my eye: 'Many new and exquisite vines may now be obtained, and among lovely things that I am open to receive from anybody (and will pay carriage) are *Vitis Thunbergii*; *Vitis Californica*, a tremendous grower;

Vitis aconitifolia, a gem from China; and *Vitis megaphylla*, most distinct of all arrivals in this family.'

My heart leaped with joy as I thought: 'Is it possible that I, even I, may contribute to Mr. Philpotts's garden?' Promptly flew out my letters to Massachusetts, to Texas, in quest of the grapes. Answers showed that at least one of them could be mine for the asking and a little besides; but before I had actually ordered the plant, as good luck would have it, I happened upon the following passage in 'My Garden,' unseen heretofore: 'Green corn is a pleasant vegetable, and I surprise Americans who come to see me, by giving them that familiar dish. Let them have but that and ice, and a squash pie, and they ask no more, but to be allowed to talk about themselves and their noble country.' Needless to say that, in so far as I can achieve it, Mr. Eden Philpotts has gone, goes, and shall go grapeless.

Louisa Yeomans King

Daisy chains and cowslip balls . . .

✦⟶⟵✦

April 3rd. – The children have been making daisy chains. There are no cowslips yet awhile for cowslip balls, and as they, like their elders, are in search of a new sensation, a fresh idea, I have been reading to them out of an old book. I bade them first take 'a small branch or long spray of the white-thorn, with all its spines uninjured, and on its alternate thorns, a white and a blue violet, plucked from their stalks, are stuck upright in succession, until the thorns are covered, and when placed in a flower-pot of moss, has perfectly the appearance of a beautiful vernal flowering dwarf shrub, and as long as it remains fresh, is an object of surprise and delight.' I think this is a pretty idea and worthy of note. I have just been teaching the children to make 'Aunt Sallies' out of great white daisies. You chip the white petals round the centre for the frill of a white cap, leaving four petals for strings at the bottom. Then with a brush you paint in eyes, nose, and mouth on the yellow centre, and you have a wonderful miniature face of an old woman. Let any child try and they are bound to be charmed with the result. Later on the big garden daisies make splendid Aunt Sallies. Daisy chains have been a joy for all time, and cowslip balls. I can remember now the joy of my first cowslip ball, only I was always sorry to pull the dear flowers to pieces. How many of us can say that youth with all its joys is with us still?

Helen Milman

THE DAISY CHAIN, *Florence Fitz-Gerald*

GARDEN FLOWERS, *Theo van Rysselberghe*

Floral arrangements in hyacinth glasses

Hyacinth glasses are also very suitable for drawing-room decoration; especially those having opaque grounds ornamented with gold. These may contain larger blooms than those mentioned for trumpet-shaped glasses, as, for example, Roses, Fuchsias, Pelargoniums, Cactuses, and others; but, associated with these, as well as with flowers of smaller sizes, should be wild Grasses, so blended as to give a light appearance to the arrangement. Oats, in a green state, as I before mentioned, are useful for this purpose, though not so light looking as ordinary Grasses; both, however, may be purchased in bunches during summer in Covent Garden, therefore, both town and country readers have an opportunity of testing their value. When flowers are about to be arranged in Hyacinth glasses, the darker and richer shades should be selected for flowers of a light colour, and lighter shades for dark flowers. A spray of such a Rose as the Duke of Edinburgh, placed in a white opaque glass embellished with gold, looks well; so does the Gloire de Dijon in a purple or dark blue glass; the arrangement in vases (if I may so term them) of this kind need not, however, be limited to one variety of flower. A white or tinted Rose, in the style of Souvenir de la Malmaison, with a spray of Dielytra, one or two blue Forget-me-nots, and a few Grasses and Ferns would form a pretty mixture. Some of these glasses may be purchased in the form of three combined . . . ; when such triplets are used, of course more flowers must be employed in their decoration, such as Roses, Lilies, Sweet Peas, Fuchsias, Pelargoniums, Dielytra, and Ferns and Grasses of various kinds. The smaller vases are well adapted for mantel-piece decoration, or for small tables. The large kinds may be placed in the centre of a table of greater size, or a group may be formed on a side table. For a small breakfast-table one of the larger-sized vases would form a pretty centre ornament with a few small specimen-glasses grouped round it.

Annie Hassard

KITCHEN GARDEN ECONOMY

Many are the complaints of the gardener against the kitchen and *vice versa*.

He says 'so much' was sent in, and the cook denies it. . . .

In many cases the pig-tub benefits and in others the 'back door.' I know an instance of a certain 'big house' that endeavoured to sell spare garden produce in the town near by. But the townspeople wouldn't buy, as they got it cheaper from the 'back door,' and after a time the plan was abandoned, to the delight of the town.

I was once called in to examine the financial side of a big garden, when the head gardener and agent showed me from their books that close on £3000 worth of fruit, vegetables, and flowers were supplied to the house in a year, proving, as they thought, that the garden paid. I pointed out that supposing fifteen people were in the house *all the year round*, even allowing an outrageous estimate of £2 per head per week, the total only amounted to £1560, and this did not even include potatoes!

Incredible, but true. Little wonder that the house and estate is for sale! The gardener and agent were quite above suspicion. Back door again! . . .

It is sometimes difficult to know what is really required in the way of potatoes. I recently inquired of a gardener how many he thought would be needed for the next six months. He replied, 'A ton.' The cook then informed me she used at the outside 5 lbs. a day, 35 lbs. a week – 56 lbs. is 1 bushel, 112 lbs. 2 bushels (1 cwt.), 20 cwt. to the ton. So half a ton was ordered! Just an error in calculation, needing five minutes to put right.

A man I knew walked round his kitchen-garden and found a quarter of an acre under onions. As they all disliked onions, he quietly arranged for their sale without saying anything first!

MRS PHILIP MARTINEAU

THE CABBAGE FIELD, *Frederick Hall*

GARDEN MAGIC

EMERALD CAVERNS

IN THE

DEPTHS OF FOLIAGE . . .

THE GARDEN, SUTTON PLACE, SURREY, *Ernest Spence*

A BLOOD-RED FLOWER

'I don't know much about love,' she said, 'and I do not like to talk of things I do not understand; but I have heard two opinions. Some say the Devil carried the seed from hell, and planted it on the earth to plague men and make them sin; and some say, that when all the plants in the garden of Eden were pulled up by the roots, one bush that the angels had planted was left growing, and it spread its seed over the whole earth, and its name is love. I do not know which is right – perhaps both. There are different species that go under the same name. There is a love that begins in the head, and goes down to the heart, and grows slowly; but it lasts till death, and asks less than it gives. There is another love, that blots out wisdom, that is sweet with the sweetness of life and bitter with the bitterness of death, lasting for an hour; but it is worth having lived a whole life for that hour. I cannot tell: perhaps the old monks were right when they tried to root love out; perhaps the poets are right when they try to water it. It is a blood-red flower, with the colour of sin; but there is always the scent of a god about it.'

Gregory would have made a remark; but she said, without noticing:

'There are as many kinds of loves as there are flowers: everlastings that never wither; speedwells that wait for the wind to fan them out of life; blood-red mountain-lilies that pour their voluptuous sweetness out for one day, and lie in the dust at night. There is no flower has the charm of all – the speedwell's purity, the everlasting's strength, the mountain-lily's warmth; but who knows whether there is no love that holds all – friendship, passion, worship?

'Such a love,' she said, in her sweetest voice, 'will fall on the surface of strong, cold, selfish life as the sunlight falls on a torpid winter world . . .'

OLIVE SCHREINER

CHOOSING, *George Frederick Watts*

PORTRAIT OF THE ARTIST'S WIFE, *Harold Harvey*

'I BE LAVIN' THE MORNIN''

✦━━◆━━✦

I write feelingly of Box edging to-day. Last week, Holy Week, I spent in the country, and most of my time was passed on my knees. For, when not at church or driving the intervening five miles, I was setting out plants in the garden, and that, like one's prayers, requires kneeling. Four men were working, setting out plants and trees, but the earth was so sweet and warm and brown that it was impossible to keep away from it. With trowel in hand and joy in my heart, I set out hundreds of little Box plants, transplanted Columbines, Foxgloves and Canterbury Bells. Big robins were hopping tamely about, calling to one another; blackbirds and meadow-larks were singing their refrains; the brave plants were pushing their way through the earth to new life, and I thought how good it was to be alive, to have a garden to dig in, and, above all, to be well and able to dig.

With work in the garden care and worry vanish. The cook (as some cooks of mine have done) may announce that "tis a woild waste of a place. I be lavin' the mornin'.' The hamper of meat does not arrive on the one train from town, or somebody smashes something very dear to your heart, – just go to the garden, tie up some Roses or vines, or poke about with a trowel, and though murder may have been in your thoughts, in half an hour serenity will return. And what does it all matter, anyway? Another maid can cook for a few days, and there are always bacon and eggs.

Philosophy is inevitably learned in a garden.

HELENA RUTHERFURD ELY

THE GARDEN

My heart shall be thy garden. Come, my own,
　　Into thy garden; thine be happy hours
　　Among my fairest thoughts, my tallest flowers,
From root to crowning petal thine alone.
Thine is the place from where the seeds are sown
　　Up to the sky enclosed, with all its showers.
　　But ah, the birds, the birds! Who shall build bowers
To keep these thine? O friend, the birds have flown.

For as these come and go, and quit our pine
　　To follow the sweet season, or, new-comers,
　　　Sing one song only from our alder-trees,
My heart has thoughts, which, though thine eyes hold mine,
　　Flit to the silent world and other summers,
　　　With wings that dip beyond the silver seas.

ALICE MEYNELL

YOUNG LOVE, *Gunning King*

THE GARDENS OF THE GENERALIFE, GRANADA, *Ludwig Hans Fischer*

THE GENERALIFE

A wonderfully peaceful place, that Alcazar garden watched over by the great Moorish lattice-work tower of the cathedral, and by its own high, slender palm trees; a *hortus inclusus* in the best sense, where the winter sun lies on the myrtle hedges and on the blue-and-green tiled paths strewn with fragrant, dry fig-leaves. In it one naturally remembers that Rhodes and Damascus – names to conjure with! – are much on the same line, and somehow seem near (with the palm trees brought from them); and one muses on serene mediæval days, learned Saracen leeches, and Jewish philosophers, verses of Omar Khayyám coming into one's head. Spanish Spain with bullfights and cigarettes, Seville of Don Juan and Figaro, has nothing to say to these Moorish gardens; has closed them in, or rather closed *them out of herself*, into peacefulness and gentle decay.

This is, of course, very much the feeling of the Generalife above Grenada. I say *its* feeling, not merely mine about it; because places like these have moods and emotions on their account, seem to feel something which they transmit to us. Only the Generalife has an added quality of romance, its terraces and hedged paths, and little porticos and fountains overhanging, in their charmed regularity, the stony, savage gorge of the Darro; overlooking the red towers and creeping walls of the Alhambra. And then, beyond, the solemn blue plain, and the peaks and everlasting snows of the Sierra.

Far more than the Alhambra itself, which savours too much of the show-place, Palace of the Cæsars or Hadrian's villa, this little Generalife has kept the poetry of Moorish Spain. Partly also because of its small size, and mainly, of course, because it is, if not inhabited, at least inhabitable, and belongs to a private individual descended in direct line from its original owners.

That is the fascination: this odd, unlikely fact, this bridging of the chasm between past and present, modern Christendom and that vanished Islam; realizing it, one feels rather as in the presence of persons intermarried with ghosts.

VERNON LEE

THE GARDENS OF FERNHAM

As I have said already that it was an October day, I dare not forfeit your respect and imperil the fair name of fiction by changing the season and describing lilacs hanging over garden walls, crocuses, tulips and other flowers of spring. Fiction must stick to facts, and the truer the facts the better the fiction – so we are told. Therefore it was still autumn and the leaves were still yellow and falling, if anything, a little faster than before, because it was now evening (seven twenty-three to be precise) and a breeze (from the south-west to be exact) had risen. But for all that there was something odd at work:

My heart is like a singing bird
   Whose nest is in a water'd shoot;
My heart is like an apple tree
   Whose boughs are bent with thick-set fruit –

perhaps the words of Christina Rossetti were partly responsible for the folly of the fancy – it was nothing of course but a fancy – that the lilac was shaking its flowers over the garden walls, and the brimstone butterflies were scudding hither and thither, and the dust of the pollen was in the air. A wind blew, from what quarter I know not, but it lifted the half-grown leaves so that there was a flash of silver grey in the air. It was the time between the lights when colours undergo their intensification and purples and golds burn in window-panes like the beat of an excitable heart; when for some reason the beauty of the world revealed and yet soon to perish (here I pushed into the garden, for, unwisely, the door was left open and no beadles seemed about), the beauty of the world which is so soon to perish, has two edges, one of laughter, one of anguish, cutting the heart asunder. The gardens of Fernham lay before me in the spring twilight, wild and open, and in the long grass, sprinkled and carelessly flung, were daffodils and bluebells, not orderly perhaps at the best of times, and now wind-blown and waving as they tugged at their roots.

VIRGINIA WOOLF

BURTON BRADSTOCK, DORSET, TOWARDS EVENING, *Hugh L. Norris*

IRISES IN THE HORIKIRI GARDENS, TOKYO, *Ella du Cane*

An Old Temple Garden in Japan

It is not around these large and world-renowned temples that one finds a garden, in the sense that we Europeans regard a garden, but rather in some peaceful spot which seems to have been overlooked by the hustle and bustle of the large town in which it may be situated. I am thinking now of one such garden in Kyoto; the evening bell seems to call you to come within its sanctuary, and once there one would surely never leave until the final closing of its great outer wooden door sends the loiterer away. It has an irresistible charm this tiny garden, hardly more than a toy compared to the scale of our English gardens, and it was no surprise to me to learn that it was planned to suggest in miniature the fabulous Garden of Paradise. One enters its outer precincts through one of those solid wooden gateways which seem so fitting to guard their charge, wood guarding wood, for remember all temples are made of wood in Japan; though many different kinds may be used, and the rarer and more beautifully veined pieces are brought together and collected from far and wide, still it is all wood, and for that reason the buildings seem to be especially in keeping with a garden.

On either side of the gateway stand two old pine-trees, carefully trained and thinned at the proper season; but the most beautiful guardian is just within the gate, a grand old weeping cherry-tree, in April its boughs bent down by the weight of its blossoms, while its glory lasts for a week or two, casting a pinky light on all around.

Florence du Cane

MAGGIE AND THE ROSE

They passed on into the conservatory.

'How strange and unreal the trees and flowers look with the lights among them,' said Maggie, in a low voice. 'They look as if they belonged to an enchanted land, and would never fade away:– I could fancy they were all made of jewels.'

She was looking at the tier of geraniums as she spoke, and Stephen made no answer; but he was looking at her – and does not a supreme poet blend light and sound into one, calling darkness mute, and light eloquent? Something strangely powerful there was in the light of Stephen's long gaze, for it made Maggie's face turn towards it and look upward at it – slowly, like a flower at the ascending brightness. And they walked unsteadily on, without feeling that they were walking – without feeling anything but that long grave mutual gaze which has the solemnity belonging to all deep human passion. The hovering thought that they must and would renounce each other made this moment of mute confession more intense in its rapture.

But they had reached the end of the conservatory, and were obliged to pause and turn. The change of movement brought a new consciousness to Maggie: she blushed deeply, turned away her head, and drew her arm from Stephen's, going up to some flowers to smell them. Stephen stood motionless, and still pale.

'O may I get this rose?' said Maggie, making a great effort to say something, and dissipate the burning sense of irretrievable confession. 'I think I am quite wicked with roses – I like to gather them and smell them till they have no scent left.'

Stephen was mute: he was incapable of putting a sentence together, and Maggie bent her arm a little upward towards the large half-opened rose that had attracted her.

GEORGE ELIOT

MY SWEET ROSE, *John William Waterhouse*

THE DOCTOR'S GARDEN

But as Nan sat in the old summer-house in the doctor's garden, she thought of many things that she must remember to tell her grandmother about this delightful day. The bees were humming in the vines, and as she looked down the wide garden-walk it seemed like the broad aisle in church, and the congregation of plants and bushes all looked at her as if she were in the pulpit. The church itself was not far away, and the windows were open, and sometimes Nan could hear the preacher's voice, and by and by the people began to sing, and she rose solemnly, as if it were her own parishioners in the garden who lifted up their voices. A cheerful robin began a loud solo in one of Dr. Leslie's cherry-trees, and the little girl laughed aloud in her make-believe meeting-house, and then the gate was opened and shut, and the doctor himself appeared, strolling along, and smiling as he came.

He was looking to the right and left at his flowers and trees, and once he stopped and took out his pocket knife to trim a straying branch of honey-suckle, which had wilted and died. When he came to the summer-house, he found his guest sitting there demurely with her hands folded in her lap. She had gathered some little sprigs of box and a few blossoms of periwinkle and late lilies of the valley, and they lay on the bench beside her. 'So you did not go to church with Marilla?' the doctor said. 'I dare say one sermon a day is enough for so small a person as you.' For Nan's part, no sermon at all would have caused little sorrow, though she liked the excitement of the Sunday drive to the village. She only smiled when the doctor spoke, and gave a little sigh of satisfaction a minute afterward when he seated himself beside her.

SARAH ORNE JEWETT

THE GARDEN, *Alfred Parsons*

IN THE GARDEN (CELIA THAYER IN HER GARDEN), 1892, *Childe Hassam*

An Island Garden

Jane had already decided that there was never a garden in the world like hers. She was crazy about it. An early, old-fashioned yellow rose-bush was already in bloom. Shadows of poppies danced here and there. The stone dike was smothered in wild-rose bushes starred with crimson bud sheaths. Pale lemon lilies and creamy June lilies grew in the corners. There was ribbon-grass and mint, bleeding-heart, prince's feather, southernwood, peonies, sweet balm, sweet may, sweet william, all with sated, velvet bees humming over them. Aunt Matilda Jollie had been content with old-fashioned perennials, and Jane loved them too, but she made up her mind that by hook or by crook she would have some annuals the next summer. At the beginning of that summer Jane was already planning for the next.

In a very short time Jane was to be full of garden lore, and was always trying to extract information about fertilizers from anybody who knew. Mr Jimmy John gravely advised well-rotted cow manure, and Jane dragged basketfuls of it home from his barnyard. She loved to water the flowers, especially when the earth was a little dry and they drooped pleadingly. The garden rewarded her; she was one of those people at whose touch things grow. No weed was ever allowed to show its face. Jane got up early every morning to weed. It was wonderful to wake as the sun came over the sea. The mornings at Lantern Hill seemed different from the mornings anywhere else – more morningish. Jane's heart sang as she weeded and raked and hoed and pruned and thinned out.

'Who taught you these things, woman?' asked Dad.

'I think I've always known them,' said Jane dreamily.

L. M. Montgomery

A MAGIC PLACE

Selden had given her his arm without speaking. She took it in silence, and they moved away, not toward the supper-room, but against the tide which was setting thither. The faces about her flowed by like the streaming images of sleep: she hardly noticed where Selden was leading her, till they passed through a glass doorway at the end of the long suite of rooms and stood suddenly in the fragrant hush of a garden. Gravel grated beneath their feet, and about them was the transparent dimness of a midsummer night. Hanging lights made emerald caverns in the depths of foliage, and whitened the spray of a fountain falling among lilies. The magic place was deserted: there was no sound but the plash of the water on the lily-pads, and a distant drift of music that might have been blown across a sleeping lake.

Selden and Lily stood still, accepting the unreality of the scene as a part of their own dream-like sensations. It would not have surprised them to feel a summer breeze on their faces, or to see the lights among the boughs reduplicated in the arch of a starry sky. The strange solitude about them was no stranger than the sweetness of being alone in it together.

At length Lily withdrew her hand, and moved away a step, so that her white-robed slimness was outlined against the dusk of the branches. Selden followed her, and still without speaking they seated themselves on a bench beside the fountain.

Suddenly she raised her eyes with the beseeching earnestness of a child. 'You never speak to me – you think hard things of me,' she murmured.

'I think of you at any rate, God knows!' he said.

'Then why do we never see each other? Why can't we be friends? You promised once to help me,' she continued in the same tone, as though the words were drawn from her unwillingly.

'The only way I can help you is by loving you,' Selden said in a low voice.

She made no reply, but her face turned to him with the soft motion of a flower.

EDITH WHARTON

108

SOLITUDE, *James Sim*

A COTTAGE GARDEN AT SUNSET, *David Woodlock*

THE SANCTUARY

She walks quickly on, between flower-borders and shrubberies, until she reaches a wrought-iron gate that leads into the walled garden. She opens it and passes through, then stands still once again to listen. She has succeeded at last. Not an echo of Betty's high-pitched indecencies attains to this quiet garden-close to offend her ears. There is no noise less clean and harmless than that of the south wind delicately wagging the heads of the slumberous flowers.

The garden, as its name implies, is hedged in from each rude gust on three sides by stout walls, stone-coped and balled. On the fourth, towards the sun-setting, it is guarded only by a light decorated iron railing, now muffled in the airy fluff of the traveller's joy, and embraced by the luxuriant arms of the hop, the clematis, and the wandering vine. Between their tendrils, between the branches of the strong tea-rose and the Virginia creeper's autumn fires, one catches friendly glimpses of the church tower and the park, and the gentle deer. Inside, the garden is encompassed by wide and crowded flower-borders, but the middle is sacred to the green simplicity of the velvet grass.

Margaret draws a deep breath of relief, and begins to walk slowly along. A row of tall, white gladioli, nearly as high-statured as herself, looking ghostly fair in the star-shine, keep her company, lovely and virginal as May lilies; and from the farther side of the garden comes an ineffable waft of that violet smell which we used to connect only with spring. As she paces to and fro the ugly din fades out of her ears, and the ireful red out of her cheeks. A sort of peace settles down upon her . . .

RHODA BROUGHTON

AFTER THE STORM

It was delicious in the garden. The storm had passed over long since, and it was still and warm; the sweetness of the stocks and roses filled the air with the peculiar intensity of fragrance of flowers after rain – in the evening light they had the unnatural shadowy vividness of a coloured photograph. The rain had stirred up the nightingales too – near and far, their bubbling ecstasy welled out from the dark shelter of ilexes and cypresses, and through the open windows of the villa there came presently the cool elusive sequences of Debussy's music – ghosts of melody rather than melodies, evocations rather than statements; gleams on water and pale lights in spring skies, a single star, slow waves beating in mist on a deserted shore. Grace leant back in the corner of her seat, listening, watching the leaves of the buckthorns, like little curved pencils, against the sky above her head; in the relaxation of fatigue her attention was fixed on nothing, but some part of her was profoundly aware of all these things – the scent of the flowers, the song of the nightingales, the cool western music, with its memories of her own Atlantic shores.

ANN BRIDGE

REFLECTIONS, *Marcel Rieder*

THE AUTHORS

Biographical information and text sources. Cuts in the extracts have been indicated by an ellipsis and the word 'edited' in the text sources below. Inverted commas round an author's name indicate a pseudonym.

LOUISA MAY ALCOTT (1832-88), novelist and reformist, was born in Pennsylvania, the eldest daughter of the improvident philosopher Bronson Alcott. With the publication of *Little Women* (1868), Louisa became the main breadwinner for the family, writing a huge number of novels, stories, poems and articles. 'Gardens for Little Women' from *Little Women*, London 1952.

'ELIZABETH' VON ARNIM (1866-1941), novelist, was born in New Zealand. *Elizabeth and her German Garden* (1898) and *The Solitary Summer* (1899) describe her life on her first husband's Pomeranian estate, an amusing combination of horticulture, child-rearing and accounts of her relationship with 'the Man of Wrath'. 'The Scented Sweet-Pea' (edited) from *The Solitary Summer*, London 1910.

'E.V.B.', ELEANOR VERE BOYLE, (fl. 1852-1908), writer and illustrator, produced books for children and whimsical works on horticulture. Her gardening books include *A Garden of Pleasure* (1895) and *Sylvana's Letters to an Unknown Friend* (1900). 'Indian Visions' from *Garden Colour*, ed. Margaret Waterfield, London 1905; 'The Garden Unconstrained' from *The Peacock's Pleasaunce*, London 1908.

'ANN BRIDGE' (1889-1974), novelist, of Anglo-American parentage, wrote to supplement her diplomat husband's income. Travels in China provided the setting for *Peking Picnic* (1932) and *The Ginger Griffin* (1934), which display her enthusiasm for travelogue and psychology. Similarly, *Illyrian Spring* (1935), set on the Dalmatian coast, combines a wistful love story with seductive descriptions of the countryside. 'After the Storm' from *Illyrian Spring*, London 1935.

RHODA BROUGHTON (1840-1920), novelist, was born in Wales and grew up in Staffordshire. *Cometh Up as a Flower* (1867) established her reputation as a daring writer, but her work appeared less outrageous as time went on: 'I began my life as Zola; I finish it as Miss Yonge.' 'The Sanctuary' (edited) from *Doctor Cupid*, London 1886.

FRANCES HODGSON BURNETT (1849-1924), novelist, short-story writer and playwright, was born in Lancashire and emigrated to Tennessee in 1865. She was established as a popular and prolific writer by the time *Little Lord Fauntleroy* appeared in 1886. *The Secret Garden* (1911) has become a children's classic. 'The Secret Garden Blooms' (edited) from *The Secret Garden*, London 1911.

BARBARA CAMPBELL (fl. 1901) married an Englishman and eventually returned with him to New England, where she took over the management of her father's garden. *The Garden of a Commuter's Wife* combines horticultural enthusiasm with vivid vignettes of her servants and gardeners. 'The Rebellious Border' from *The Garden of a Commuter's Wife*, New York and London 1911.

FLORENCE DU CANE (fl. 1908-13) wrote books about gardens in Japan, Madeira, the Canary Islands and on the Nile, beautifully illustrated with watercolours by the now forgotten artist Ella du Cane. 'Perfumed Gardens in Madeira' from *The Flowers and Gardens of Madeira*, London 1909; 'An Old Temple Garden in Japan' from *The Flowers and Gardens of Japan*, London 1908.

EDITH L. CHAMBERLAIN and FANNY DOUGLAS (fl. 1892) collaborated on *The Gentlewoman's Book of Gardening*, a practical approach to horticulture giving advice on a range of activities, including gardening as a profession for women. 'The Gentle Art of Distillation' from *The Gentlewoman's Book of Gardening*, London 1892.

ELIZA COOK (1817-89), poet and editor, was born in London and largely self-educated. Her often sentimental poetry had a wide readership including in America, and from 1849-54 she edited *Eliza Cook's Journal*, a periodical publishing verse and topical essays. 'Blue-Bells in the Shade' from *The Poetical Works of Eliza Cook*, London 1870.

MARION CRAN (1875-1942), writer and gardener, was born in South Africa. A varied career included hospital work, art journalism, and reporting on migration in the British Empire. Most attractive of gardening writers, she published prolifically, combining horticulture with personal anecdote. 'Peter Learns to Bud Roses' (edited) and 'An Embarrassment of Daffodils' from *The Story of My Ruin*, London 1924.

'E. M. DELAFIELD' (1890-1943), novelist, playwright and journalist, was born in Monmouthshire. Her novels reveal close observation of the lives of upper-middle-class and 'county' women, most famously recorded in the 'Provincial Lady' series, based on articles for Lady Rhondda's feminist *Time and Tide*. 'The Bulbs Arrive' from *The Diary of a Provincial Lady*, London 1930.

MARGARET DELAND (1857-1945), novelist, short-story writer and poet, was born in Pennsylvania. Her controversial first novel, *John Ward, Preacher* (1888) was criticized as an attack on religion. Her prime concern, however, was personal morality rather than social reform. 'The Old Garden' (edited) from *The Old Garden and Other Verses*, Boston and New York 1886.

EMILY DICKINSON (1830-86) lived reclusively at her family home in Amherst, Massachusetts. Regarded today as a major American poet, she wrote nearly 1800 poems, but only a handful were published in her lifetime. 'I Tend My Flowers for Thee' from *The Complete Poems of Emily Dickinson*, Thomas H. Johnson, ed., London 1975.

THERESA (MRS. C. W.) EARLE (1836-1925), gardener, writer and vegetarian, after art training and a career as wife and mother, achieved fame in her sixties with her 'Pot-Pourri' books, a charming melange of gardening tips, recipes, reminiscences, hints on reading, and views on the education of women. 'An Old-Fashioned Garden' from *Pot-Pourri from a Surrey Garden*, London 1897.

'GEORGE ELIOT' (1819-80) was an outstanding Victorian novelist. Characterized by complex psychological exploration and social realism, her novels achieved critical and popular acclaim. Virginia Woolf described her as 'one of the first English novelists to discover that men and women think as well as feel'. References to flowers and gardens appear in her fiction and poetry, often recalling her Warwickshire childhood. 'Maggie and the Rose' from *The Mill on the Floss*, Edinburgh and London 1860.

HELENA RUTHERFURD ELY (1858-1920), gardener and writer, grew up in New Jersey. Her first book, *A Woman's Hardy Garden* (1903), had a revolutionary impact on American gardening, proposing the cultivation of perennials and naturally grown annuals instead of the ubiquitous bedding-out system. 'I Be Lavin' the Mornin'' from *A Woman's Hardy Garden*, New York 1903.

ELIZABETH GASKELL (1810-65), novelist, short-story writer, biographer and conversationalist, grew up in Cheshire. A productive writer, she also raised four daughters and engaged in social reform. Her long working relationship with Dickens once provoked the famous outburst: 'Mrs Gaskell – fearful – fearful! If I were Mr G. O Heaven how I would beat her!' References to flowers, gardens and the countryside abound in her works, often providing a sympathetic commentary on the action. 'A Visit to the Towers Gardens' from *Wives and Daughters*, London 1866.

The sole known work of ANNIE HASSARD (fl. 1875) is her practical guide to arranging plants and flowers in the home, which ranges from the formal showpiece to bouquets and buttonholes, with advice on appropriate lighting and the right kind of container. 'Floral Arrangements in Hyacinth Glasses' (edited) from *Floral Decorations for the Dwelling House*, London 1875.

GERTRUDE JEKYLL (1843-1932), artist, photographer, craftswoman, gardener and writer, revolutionized English gardening with her innovative approach to garden design and the cultivation and use of plants. 'Making Garden Pictures' from *Colour in the Flower Garden*, London 1908; 'Hollyhocks' from *Some English Gardens* (with George S. Elgood), London 1904; 'Gardening Tools for Children' from *Children and Gardens*, London 1908.

SARAH ORNE JEWETT (1849-1909), novelist and short-story writer, grew up in Berwick, Maine. She wrote about women, particularly in rural communities, exploring the subtle and powerful emotions that often underlie apparently simple lives. 'Miss Sydney's Flowers' from *Old Friends and New*, Boston 1879; 'The Doctor's Garden' from *A Country Doctor*, Boston 1884.

LOUISA YEOMANS (MRS FRANCIS) KING (1863-1948), gardener and writer, grew up in New Jersey. Influenced by her mother-in-law and by Gertrude Jekyll's revolutionary ideas, Louisa King gardened, wrote extensively on gardening, and helped to found the Garden Club of America. 'An Anglo-American Encounter' from *The Well-Considered Garden*, London 1916.

ROSE G. KINGSLEY (fl. 1886-1910) published a number of works on the subjects of history, art, travel and gardening. 'The Accommodating Rhododendron' from *Eversley Gardens and Others*, London 1907.

'VERNON LEE' (1856-1935), novelist and essayist, travelled widely in Europe as a child, and finally settled in Italy. Her work includes studies in aesthetics and Italian culture, novels and short stories, and essays, which often focus on what she called the *genius loci*, the essential spirit of a place. The American writer, Edith Wharton, described Lee as 'the first highly cultivated and brilliant woman I had ever known.' 'The Generalife' from *The Enchanted Woods*, London and New York 1905.

KATHERINE MANSFIELD (1888-1923), short-story writer, was born in New Zealand, and educated in Wellington and London. Her stories reflect the ebb and flow of human relationships, focusing on moments of intense emotion or consciousness. 'Life Like a Wind' from 'At the Bay' in *The Garden Party*, London 1922; 'The Pear Tree' from 'Bliss' in *Bliss and other stories*, London 1920.

MRS PHILIP MARTINEAU (fl. 1913-38) published a number of books on cookery and gardening. 'Kitchen Garden Economy' reveals her practical, no-nonsense approach: (edited) from *The Secrets of Many Gardens*, London 1924.

ANNA LEA MERRITT (1844-1930), artist, writer and gardener, was born in Philadelphia, but lived in England from the 1870s. Known primarily as an artist, she turned to gardening later in life, writing and illustrating a delightful account of her garden in Hampshire. 'Character in Flowers' from *An Artist's Garden*, London 1910.

ALICE MEYNELL (1847-1922), poet, essayist and critic, was born in London. A prolific writer, she also brought up a large family and ran a hospitable household, entertaining the Victorian literary establishment. 'The Garden' from *The Poems of Alice Meynell*, London 1940.

HELEN MILMAN (fl. 1890-1908) published her *Kalendar* in 1903: a yearbook of garden lore, quotations about plants and flowers, accounts of the weather and her day-by-day responses to nature. 'Daisy Chains and Cowslip Balls . . .' from *My Kalendar of Country Delights*, London and New York 1903.

L. M. MONTGOMERY (1874-1942), novelist and short-story writer, was born on Prince Edward Island. Her most famous novel, *Anne ('with an 'e'') of Green Gables* (1908), typically features a lively and sensitive heroine and draws a seductive picture of growing up on 'the Island'. 'An Island Garden' from *Jane of Lantern Hill*, London 1937.

KATHLEEN L. MURRAY (fl. 1914-38) wrote an attractive account of gardens that she cultivated while living in Behar and 'in the wilderness' in India. 'French Roses in an Indian Garden' from *My Garden in the Wilderness*, London, Calcutta and Simla 1914(?).

MRS RICHMOND (fl. 1908) was Garden Editor of the *Queen* and wrote a number of gardening books. *In My Lady's Garden* takes the reader through the gardening year with week-by-week advice. 'A Traditional Potpourri' from *In My Lady's Garden*, London and Leipsic 1908.

ELEANOUR SINCLAIR ROHDE (*c.*1881-1950) was born in Alleppey, southern India and educated at Cheltenham Ladies' College and St Hilda's Hall, Oxford. A prolific writer on gardening and garden lore, with a particular interest in early gardening and herbs, her books combine practical information with a wealth of historical detail. Rohde's scholarship and achievements were widely recognized, and she became President of the Society of Women Journalists. 'Great-Aunt Lancilla's Scented Garden' from *The Scented Garden*, London 1931.

CHRISTINA ROSSETTI (1830-94), poet and short-story writer, was born in London of Anglo-Italian parents. A superb technician with an immense lyric gift, she wrote most powerfully about love, loss and resignation. Flowers are often used symbolically in her poetry. 'Golden Glories' from *A Pageant and Other Poems*, London 1881.

VITA SACKVILLE-WEST (1892-1962), poet, novelist, biographer, travel writer and gardener, was brought up at Knole in Kent. Perhaps most remembered for the garden she created at Sissinghurst with her husband Harold Nicolson, she recorded her love of the English countryside and gardens in two long poems, *The Land* (1926) and *The Garden* (1946). 'The Island' from *The Land*, London 1926.

OLIVE SCHREINER (1855-1920), novelist, essayist and reformer, was born in South Africa. *The Story of an African Farm* (1883) explores moral idealism and feminism through its two main protagonists and suggests that, to attain conventional adult relationships, both these aspirations must be sacrificed. 'A Blood-Red Flower' (edited) from *The Story of an African Farm*, London 1893 edition.

EDITH WHARTON (1862-1937), novelist, short-story and travel writer, and architectural essayist, was born in New York and travelled widely in Europe as a child. Her novels depict the stifling and sometimes fatal effects of social convention, particularly on the lives of women. 'A Magic Place' from *The House of Mirth*, London and New York 1905.

FRANCES GARNET WOLSELEY (1872-1936), gardener, teacher and reformer, founded the Glynde College for Lady Gardeners in Sussex on the principle that women working on the land encouraged female emancipation and was beneficial to society, a philosophy that found particular resonance during the First World War. 'The Essential Gardening Hat' from *Gardening for Women*, London 1908.

VIRGINIA WOOLF (1882-1941), writer and reader, was an innovative thinker and technician, experimenting in fiction with new ways of using language and structure to pin down experience. Her feminist essays, such as *Three Guineas* (1938), continue to stimulate debate. 'Walking in Kew Gardens' from *Kew Gardens*, London 1927; 'The Gardens of Fernham' from *A Room of One's Own*, London 1931.

The publisher would like to thank the following for permission to reproduce extracts: 'After the Storm' from *Illyrian Spring* by Ann Bridge, reprinted by permission of the Peters, Fraser & Dunlop Group Ltd; 'I Tend My Flowers for Thee' reprinted by permission of the publishers and the Trustees of Amherst College from *The Poems of Emily Dickinson*, Thomas H. Johnson, ed., Cambridge, Mass.: The Belknap Press of Harvard University Press, Copyright 1951 © 1955, 1979, 1983, by the President and Fellows of Harvard College; 'An Anglo-American Encounter', reprinted courtesy of B.T. Batsford Ltd, and with the permission of Charles Scribner's Sons, an imprint of Macmillan Publishing Company, from *The Well-Considered Garden* by Mrs Francis King, Copyright 1915, 1922 Charles Scribner's Sons; copyright renewed 1943, 1950 Mrs Louisa Yeomans King; 'Great-Aunt Lancilla's Garden' from *The Scented Garden* by Eleanour Sinclair Rohde, reprinted by permission of The Medici Society; 'The Island' from *The Land* by Vita Sackville-West, reprinted by permission of Nigel Nicolson.

Every effort has been made to trace holders of copyright. The publisher will be pleased to hear from any persons or organizations who are holders of such copyright, and will make amendments for omissions in future editions.

⚜

ACKNOWLEDGEMENTS

The editor would like to thank the following for their generous assistance with researching this book: Christopher Wood, Dr Brent Elliott and his colleagues at the Royal Horticultural Society Lindley Library, the staff at the British Library, Miranda Dewar of the Bridgeman Art Library, Linda Hammerbeck of Fine Art Photographs, and Sara Brinkhurst for botanical advice. Thanks are also due to Vivien Bowler and Janet Ravenscroft at Little, Brown, to David Fordham for designing the book and Nadine Wickenden for her decorative illustrations.

The publisher would like to thank the following museums, galleries and individuals for supplying illustrations:

ARTOTHEK: p96 The Gardens of the Generalife, Granada, *Ludwig Hans Fischer*.

BRIDGEMAN ART LIBRARY: pp2-3 A Summer Herbaceous Border, *Lilian Stannard*, Christopher Wood Gallery, London (hereafter abbreviated to CWG); pp12-13 In the Pleasaunce, Knostrop Old Hall, Leeds, *John Atkinson Grimshaw*, Christie's, London; p15 Among the Flowers, *Robert Payton Reid*, Anthony Mitchell Fine Paintings, Nottingham; p16 Lilies, Delphiniums and Poppies in the Garden of the Artist's Cottage, *Edward Kington Brice*, CWG; p19 Girl under a Parasol, *P. Lira*, Whitford & Hughes, London; p21 Madonna Lilies, *Mildred Anne Butler*, Chris Beetles Ltd, London; p29 Sun and Moon Flowers, *George Dunlop Leslie*, Guildhall Art Gallery, Corporation of London; p30 A Mediterranean Garden, *Tom Mostyn*, Christie's, London; p33 A Herbaceous Border, *Hugh L. Norris*, CWG; p35 The Poppy Garden, *Maurice Bompard*, Josef Mensing Gallery, Hamm-Rhynern; p36 The Garden Path, *Ernest Walbourn*, Phillips, The International Fine Art Auctioneers; pp38-9 At Dunster, *Arthur Claude Strachan*, Chris Beetles Ltd; p41 Summer, 1917, *Harold Harvey*, Bonhams, London; p42 A Bypath, *Mildred Anne Butler*, Bonhams, London; p48 The Pear Orchard, *Alfred Parsons*, Falmouth Art Gallery, Cornwall; p57 Asleep among the Foxgloves, *Sidney Shelton*, Waterhouse and Dodd, London; p66 Feeding the Doves, *Edmond Alphonse Defonte*, Josef Mensing Gallery, Hamm-Rhynern; p69 The Bey's Garden, 1865, *John Frederick Lewis*, Harris Museum & Art Gallery, Preston, Lancashire; p71 The Little Gardener, *Harold Swanwick*, Chris Beetles Ltd; p76 Raundscliffe – Everywhere are Roses, *George Samuel Elgood*, CWG; p79 The Herbaceous Border, *Alfred John Billinghurst*, Private Collection; p80 Flowers on the Terrace, *Victor Gilsoul*, Berko Fine Paintings, Knokke-Zoute; p84 Garden Flowers, *Theo van Rysselberghe*, Christie's, London; p99 Burton Bradstock, Dorset, Towards Evening, *Hugh. L. Norris*, Bonhams, London; p103 My Sweet Rose, *John William Waterhouse*, Roy Miles Gallery, 29 Bruton Street, London W1; p105 The Garden, *Alfred Parsons*, Trustees of the Royal Watercolour Society, London; p106 In the Garden (Celia Thayer in her Garden), 1892, *Childe Hassam*, National Museum of American Art, Smithsonian Institute; p109 Solitude, *James Sim*, Gavin Graham Gallery, London.

CHRISTOPHER WOOD GALLERY: p47 Blyborough, Lincolnshire, 1901, *George Samuel Elgood*.

FINE ART PHOTOGRAPHS: p22 In the Park, *Caroline van Deurs*, Waterhouse & Dodd, London; p25 In the Garden, *David Woodlock*, Cooper Fine Arts; p26 The Garden at Escrick Hall, Yorkshire, 1921, *Constance Wenlock*; p51 The Rose Bush, *Christine Marie Lovmand*, Christopher Cole Fine Paintings; p52 A Pretty Cottage Garden, *Alfred Augustus Glendening*, Barn Gallery; p55 Springtime in the Woods, *George Henry*, Anthony Mitchell Paintings, Nottingham; p58 A Flowery Glade, *Alfred Parsons*, courtesy of Mr Fulda; p61 In the Conservatory, *Jacques Joseph Tissot*; p62-3 A Cottage Garden, *John Horner*, Cooper Fine Arts, London; p65 Pruning Roses, *Robert James Gordon*; p72 Tending the Nasturtiums, *A. Templeuve*; p75 Picking Hyacinths, Springtime, *Arthur Herbert Buckland*, Baumkotter Gallery; p83 The Daisy Chain, *Florence Fitz-Gerald*, Christopher Cole Paintings, Beaconsfield; p87 The Cabbage Field, *Frederick Hall*, © Barbara Hall; pp88-9 The Garden, Sutton Place, Surrey, *Ernest Spence*, Anthony Mitchell Paintings, Nottingham; p92 Portrait of the Artist's Wife, *Harold Harvey*; p95 Young Love, *Gunning King*, Roger Widdas Fine Paintings, Solihull; p100 Irises in the Horikiri Gardens, Tokyo, *Ella du Cane*; p110 A Cottage Garden at Sunset, *David Woodlock*, Harper Fine Paintings; p113 Reflections, *Marcel Rieder*, Richmond Gallery.

© MANCHESTER CITY ART GALLERIES: p45 and jacket (detail), Girl Reading, *Charles Edward Perugini*.

NATIONAL PORTRAIT GALLERY: p91 Choosing, *George Frederick Watts*.